BOY'S BOOK

OF

TURTLES AND LIZARDS

PERCY A. MORRIS

Chief Preparator
Peabody Museum of Natural History, New Haven

THE RONALD PRESS COMPANY • NEW YORK

Library of Congress Catalog Card Number: 59-12121

PRINTED IN THE UNITED STATES OF AMERICA

PREFACE

The world of natural history has sometimes been compared to reading a big book and never being able to finish its pages. Each day spent in enjoyable field observation adds still another page, filled with interesting experiences and often with surprising facts. Studying our turtles and lizards is fascinating and in many ways can be quite rewarding. There is still much to be learned about them, and nature-minded persons, both youths and adults, who have observing eyes and plenty of patience stand a good chance of discovering some new fact about these interesting animals.

This book describes the turtles and lizards to be found in the United States. Most of them are illustrated by photographs taken in their natural surroundings. The known geographic limits of each animal's range are given plus a careful description of its distinctive colors and markings, structure, average and maximum size, choice of habitat and food, reproductive practices, and natural enemies—all of the interesting facts that, collectively, make up what we now know of its natural history. Some turtles and lizards make excellent pets, and there are instructions on the care of those which do well in a home terrarium.

For help in preparing the following pages, the author is indebted to many friends who have given invaluable aid, particularly in obtaining specimens for study and photographic purposes. In particular, grateful acknowledgment is due Ralph Morrill, Edward Migdalski, David Parsons, Charles Alderman, Stephen Mroz, and Arthur Bischoff, all of the Peabody Museum of Natural History, Yale University.

For those who may be interested, most of the photographs were taken with a single-lens reflex camera, using 35-millimeter film.

PERCY A. MORRIS

New Haven, Connecticut
  June, 1959

iii

953125

CONTENTS

BOY'S BOOK
OF
TURTLES AND LIZARDS

1

THE TURTLES

SURELY there are few intelligent persons to whom a live turtle does not appeal. From the small mud turtle of the local mill pond to the marine monsters of the Gulf Stream, and from the complacent box turtle to the dime-store terrapin, the range in size and form and habit is very great. There is something about these odd relics of past ages that excites our curiosity and, in many cases, our admiration. When it comes to considering our reptiles most of us, I am afraid, abhor the snakes and merely tolerate the lizards; but we regard the turtle clan with something akin to sympathy and respect.

"Relics of the past" is not an inappropriate term, for their history goes back millions of years to the days of the dinosaurs. The earliest evidence of reptile life is found in rocks of the coal-bearing periods, at an estimated age of 240 million years. At the start of the Mesozoic Era, in what the geologists call the Triassic Period, the earth was populated by strange creatures, many of them larger and different from anything on earth today. All, however, were cold-blooded, and were either reptiles or amphibians; and it was to be millions of years before the first bird or mammal appeared. This period of our earth's history is called the "Age of Reptiles." Eventually the dinosaurs and many of their contemporaries died out and were replaced by warm-blooded animals that were better able to cope with changing climates.

The turtles, already well established during Triassic times, refused to follow the general pattern and become extinct. Instead, they have continued on to the present day essentially the same as they were some 200 million years ago. Apparently, in their evolution, they had arrived at a stage that was highly efficient for living under varying conditions; and they have plodded contentedly down the corridor of time from that day to now, practically without change.

Somewhere along the line, some group of lizard-like creatures developed into primitive birds that eventually gave us the feathered hosts we know today. The first mammals appeared, to spread all over the world and wind up with such diverse creatures as whales, mice, elephants, and man. The bony fishes, originally exclusively marine, spawned cousins that learned to live in fresh water, and proceeded to invade and populate every river, stream, creek, and lake. During all these great developments our turtles, having hit on a good thing, found no reason to change their ways and today are essentially the same as their ancestors of 200 million years ago.

Probably their greatest achievement was the success in getting their pelvic bones inside their ribs, and thus they were able to develop the protective shell. Turtles are among the few animals that carry their houses about with them. Among the invertebrates this is not uncommon, as witness the snails and clams; but, with the exception of the armadillo, the turtle is about the only vertebrate creature that is provided with a protective armor wherever it goes. Although there has been no fundamental change over the centuries, it must be admitted that they grew them bigger in the old days. The Cretaceous *Archelon,* a sea-going monster of the past, was considerably larger than any marine form living today, although some of the giant land tortoises of the Galapagos stack up well against any fossil of terrestrial habits so far found.

Figure 1. *Archelon,* probably the world's largest turtle. It lived during the Cretaceous Age, a million years ago. This is a view of the ventral (lower) side of a specimen found in South Dakota in 1895. It measures 10 feet 10 inches in length and 12 feet between the front flippers.

The distinguishing feature of this group, and the one which in fact enables us to recognize them at first glance, is their possession of a complete bony case, within which the head and limbs can generally be more or less completely retracted. This case consists of two large parts, each covered by a number of shields in most cases. The upper one, which is more or less convex, is known as the "carapace," while the lower one, which is flat or concave, is called the "plastron." These two "shells" are united at their lateral margins by a "bridge," leaving an opening at the front and at the back for the protrusion of the head, tail, and limbs.

The shell is an integral part of the turtle, formed by a fusion of the ribs; and it is impossible to remove a specimen from its shell without resorting to butchery, in spite of the old and cruel tales that a turtle could be made to crawl out of its shell by applying hot water or by placing the animal on a hot stove. We might as well expect one of us to get out of our skeleton under the same circumstances.

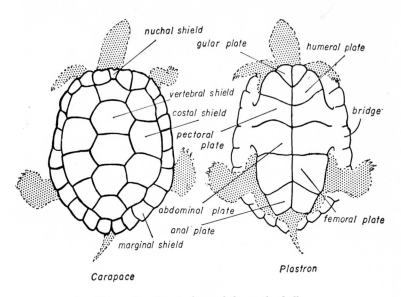

Figure 2.   Terminology of the turtle shell.

Both the carapace and plastron are bony structures, but in the majority of turtles the bone is overlaid by horny shields or plates. Generally those on the upper shell are called "shields" and those on the lower shell "plates," and they are all named. Those along the back, at the center of the carapace, are the vertebral shields; those at the sides are the costal shields; and the small ones around the edge of the shell are called marginal shields. On the plastron they are, from front to back, the gular, humeral, pectoral, abdominal, femoral, and anal plates. See Figures 2 and 3 for this terminology.

In their general internal structure the turtles agree pretty closely with the other reptiles. The lungs are of large size and extend far into the body cavity; but as the ribs

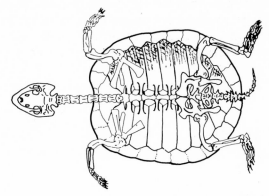

Figure 3.   Skeleton of a turtle, with plastron removed.

are immovable, respiration is accomplished by a process analogous to swallowing. The tongue is short, fleshy, and completely movable; the ears are generally quite visible; and the eyes are well formed and furnished with movable lids. The turtle has no teeth, but its beak is covered by a horny sheath with very sharp cutting edges at the sides of the jaws, and it is well equipped for cutting and tearing its food into pieces small enough to be swallowed.

Some species, such as the snapping turtle, are chiefly carnivorous; some, like the box turtle, are mainly vegetable eaters. Many are omnivorous, feeding upon both vegetable and animal matter, and nearly all of the aquatic varieties are scavengers to the extent they will not pass up a bit of carrion.

In terrestrial species the feet are commonly club shaped, the digits grouped together and only externally discernible by the claws. Fresh-water varieties, in contrast, have the digits distinct and more or less connected by a web. Marine turtles have the digits all bound together in the form of broad flippers, with the number of claws reduced. All turtles are egg layers, and all lay their eggs on land. Even the marine forms come ashore at the proper season for that purpose.

Many of the group are sluggish and inactive animals, the

slowness of the terrestrial varieties being proverbial. In
the water many of them are far from awkward or languid.
All turtles are exceedingly tenacious of life, and will live
for an unbelievably long time without any nourishment.
They will even continue to show signs of life for some time
after they have been deprived of their heads. Turtles are
also noted for their longevity. Some of the large land tortoises live to the greatest age attained by any living creature now on earth.

Of late there has been a steady increase in the sale of
baby turtles in pet shops and five-and-dime stores, and they
appear to be almost as popular for the home aquarium as
goldfish. Most of those offered for sale are newly hatched
young of the red-eared turtle, *Pseudemys scripta elegans*.
If properly cared for, these hardy little reptiles will live for
years, although in cramped quarters they will not grow very
fast and will never attain the size of their wild brothers and
sisters.

Probably the best sort of receptacle to keep them in is a
small rectangular glass aquarium. Half or more of the
bottom should be given over to a two- or three-inch water
dish, giving them ample room to swim, and the rest of the
bottom can be built up with sand and pebbles to form a

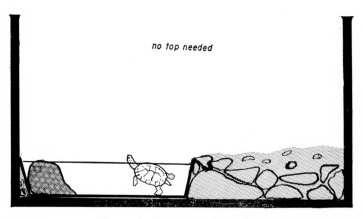

no top needed

Figure 4.   Basic cage for turtles.

sort of "beach." This is a much better arrangement than simply pouring water into the aquarium and then placing a stone in the middle for them to climb out on.

The pet stores all sell "turtle food," which is generally dried and chopped insects; but your pets will eat chopped fish, hamburg, and almost any small insect or worm dropped into the water. They will also eat lettuce as a rule, so it is no problem to give them a variety of foodstuffs. If you want to provide a special treat some day, place a few small pond snails in their water dish and watch them crush and swallow them, shells and all. Many turtles seem unable to swallow unless their heads are under water, and nearly all of them will drag their food into the water before eating it. This is bound to foul things up, so the water should be changed often. Occasionally, it is a good plan to add a little lime water to their dish, especially if you live in a "soft-water" location; about a tablespoon to a quart of water will be about right. This will aid in forming a firm shell.

Since turtles can go for a long time without any food, an occasional fasting appears to be good for them. If you are going on a vacation for a week or two, it will not be necessary to take your turtles over to "Aunt Martha's" or talk one of your neighbors into coming in to feed them every day. Make sure they have plenty of water and leave them alone. When you get back you will find them in very good shape, perhaps a little hungry, but probably more lively than ever.

Some stores sell baby turtles that have had their shells enamelled in various colors, usually with an initial or name painted on the top. Avoid these garish specimens, for the paint causes deformation of the shell and they seldom live very long. The natural colors of these diminutive examples of turtledom are far more attractive, anyway.

The names "turtle," "tortoise," and "terrapin," have been used so indiscriminately in referring to these reptiles that they are all but useless as distinctive titles. It has often been proposed that the name "tortoise" be restricted to forms that live entirely on land, "turtle" to those that live in the sea, and that "terrapin" be applied only to fresh-water varieties.

This seems to be an excellent arrangement, but even so the mixture is mischievously confusing. The name "terrapin" will probably always be used for market varieties, including marine species; the land-going box tortoise bears the scientific name *Terrapene;* and the only species that produces "tortoise shell" is a salt-water turtle! To most of us the name "turtle" means but one thing, and we shall use that throughout this book.

MUSK TURTLE

Sternotherus odoratus (Latreille)

The musk turtle is a big-headed, scrappy little fellow, looking very much like a miniature snapping turtle. It is found throughout the eastern United States, from Canada to the Gulf of Mexico, and westward into Missouri and Texas.

This is a small species, only three or four inches in length. The carapace is somewhat oblong in outline, narrower at the front end, and arched to a considerable degree. In young specimens it is distinctly keeled, but the keel disappears as the turtle grows to maturity, and adult shells are quite smooth. The plastron is small, not nearly covering the fleshy parts, and with lobes that are very feebly movable. The head is ridiculously large for so small a shell, and the feet are small but strongly webbed.

In color the shell is a dull, lusterless brown or black, sometimes faintly mottled, but it is generally so plastered with mud and algal growths that even these colors are obscured. The plastron is yellowish gray. The head and neck are black or deep greenish black. There are two prominent yellow stripes on each side of the head, running from the snout to the neck, one passing over, and one beneath, the eye.

This species has many popular names: among them "stinking turtle," "stinkpot," and "stink Jim." Even its scientific name, *odoratus,* certainly indicates that the animal is ill smelling, to say the least. A pair of inguinal glands secretes a strong and penetrating odor of musk when the reptile is handled, but in reality the odor is not as unpleasant as the turtle's unsavory names would suggest.

The musk turtle is not at all fussy about its habitat and appears equally at home in rivers, lakes, and small ponds, just so long as there is permanent water. It is a rather poor swimmer but well adapted for walking over the bottom; and it is thoroughly aquatic, coming ashore only for the purpose of egg laying. It is rarely seen sunning itself above the water line, like most of the pond turtles, but seems content to float just below the surface with merely the tip of its nose protruding. The late Dr. Ditmars of the Bronx Zoo in New York tells of confining an example in a jar of water where the turtle could rise to the surface for air but could get no purchase there so that it had to maintain itself by physical effort. Under this condition a painted turtle or a "slider" would drown in a day or two; but the musk turtle simply rose to the surface periodically, took a gulp of air, and then sank back to its preferred place at the bottom of the jar. It remained hale and hearty for several weeks and could undoubtedly have continued indefinitely living that way. In late May it is common to see large numbers gathered in shallow water, where they lie basking in the sun, but just beneath the surface.

Musk turtles are chiefly carnivorous, although they consume some vegetable matter. They are able to swallow out of water, and captive specimens usually eat freely on land; but in the wild state they roam over the muddy bottoms in search of dead animal matter, as well as any living organism they may be capable of overpowering. Small fish, newts, tadpoles, and insect larvae make up the bulk of their diet. A specimen sometimes picks up a worm and finds itself on the end of some astonished fisherman's line. This generally means a severed head, a lost hook, and one less musk turtle in that particular pond.

Egg laying takes place in the spring in the southern parts of its range, and from May to August in the north. The number of eggs is small, usually no more than five, and often only one or two. They are hard shelled with a pebbled white surface. The excavation for the eggs is always near the water, for this species does not believe in wandering afar. Commonly a site is selected at the edge of some fallen log or among the tangled roots at the base of a tree. In the Middle West this turtle often deposits its eggs in the rotten wood in the tops of stumps standing at the margin of a lake.

The musk turtle is a rugged and hardy individual to keep in the home terrarium, but far less interesting than many other species. It is reported to bite savagely, although it calms down rather quickly and becomes quite docile. Its jaws are large, however, out of all proportion to the size of the creature's body; so it is undoubtedly wise to use a little care in handling this fellow.

MISSISSIPPI MUSK TURTLE

Sternotherus carinatus (Gray)

This is a turtle of the lower Mississippi Valley. It occurs from central Arkansas and eastern Oklahoma south to the coast in Louisiana and well down into the state of Texas along the Gulf Coast. It is the largest member of the genus in this country, some individuals attaining a length of nearly six inches, although the average shell-length is about four and one-half inches.

The carapace is highly elevated at the middle, where there is a sharp dorsal keel, and from that the shell slopes rather steeply to the sides. This distinct keel gives the turtle its specific name, *carinatus*. The plastron is relatively small, as in the common musk turtle, and its lobes are weakly movable. The shell's color is light brown, usually with streaks and splashes of darker hue; but it is often so covered by mosses and algal growths that one needs to give it a good scrubbing in order to see any color at all. The plastron is yellowish gray. The head and limbs are yellowish brown with small dark spots. Like the common musk turtle, just discussed, the head is quite large and robust for the size of

Figure 5. Mississippi musk turtle.

the rest of the animal; and this species has a chin that is decorated with two dangling barbels. There are no longitudinal yellow stripes on the sides of the head.

This is chiefly a turtle of the sluggish backwaters and swampy lagoons of the lower Mississippi region. It appears to shun the swifter streams and is usually not common in the lakes or larger ponds. Give it a spread of shallow water on some floodplain, surrounded by a reed-choked marsh, and it is quite happy and content. Its food is much the same as that of the widespread common musk turtle: any fish, tadpole, or small salamander it can catch, along with worms, crustaceans, insect larvae, and what carrion it finds as it roams over the muddy and weedy bottoms.

MUD TURTLE

Kinosternon subrubrum (Lacepede)

The common mud turtle is found from southern New York and Long Island south to the northern sections of Florida. It ranges west to the Mississippi River in the southern half of the country and north to southern Illinois and Indiana. It is not known to occur in Ohio or West Virginia and has not been reported from any of the New England states, although it may possibly occur in southern Connecticut.

Figure 6.   Mud turtle.

This is a small species, seldom exceeding four inches in length. It closely resembles the common musk turtle, with which it is often confused. The shell is oval and moderately elevated, highest toward the rear, with the sides evenly rounded. The slope from the top of the carapace to the rear end is rather abrupt. Young specimens show a dorsal keel, but in mature turtles the carapace is quite smooth. The plastron is large, nearly as large as the carapace, and the two are joined by very sturdy bridges.

Perhaps the most apparent difference between the mud and the musk turtles is in the plastron. With the musk turtle this is relatively small, exposing much of the fleshy parts of the reptile; but with the mud turtle the plastron is large and partially hinged across its middle so that it can be drawn upward to protect the head and limbs. This feature is not nearly as efficient as that found in the box turtle, but it differs noticeably from the lower shell of the musk turtle. The individual shields, or plates, of the plastron are usually heavily marked by growth rings. The mud turtle's head is also large in relation to the rest of him, and its limbs are comparatively small.

In color the shell is dull brown, the margins of each shield sometimes being outlined with black; but a specimen usually needs to be scrubbed off in order to reveal any color at all because the persistently aquatic habits of this turtle leave it heavily coated with moss and mud. The plastron is dull yellowish, the growth lines strongly marked by brown. The head and neck are thickly speckled with greenish yellow; and this speckling, in place of the longitudinal stripes, forms another point of difference between this and the musk turtle.

The haunts of this turtle are many and varied. It shows a dislike for deep or swift water but is at home in a shallow pond, a sluggish stream, a weedy swamp, or a muddy ditch. Its chief desire appears to be a soft, muddy environment where there is an abundance of vegetation. It is not as strictly aquatic as the musk turtle and frequently prowls about on land. It has been observed many times in brackish salt marshes. It is not particularly fond of sunning itself other than to lie placidly in water only an inch or so deep, with its back high and dry.

In food habits they are chiefly carnivorous, for various kinds of insects, caterpillars, and crustaceans make up a large part of their diet. They will eat any dead animal matter they chance upon and undoubtedly add small mollusks and worms to their bill of fare. Captive specimens will accept almost anything that is offered them, but they ordinarily care little for vegetable matter. It is likely that in the wild state this species will eat just about anything it can catch.

The mud turtle also possesses glands that produce a disagreeable odor when the animal is handled, but it is not as pungent as that of the musk turtle.

STRIPED MUD TURTLE

Kinosternon bauri (Garman)

This turtle takes the place of the common mud turtle, *subrubrum*, in southern Florida. It is about the same size as the common form but with a lower and broader carapace that is characterized by three longitudinal paler streaks on a muddy brown background. The head also bears a pair of light-colored stripes on each side that extend well back on the neck. This species prefers small muddy ponds and ditches and frequently goes on overland forays, particularly on rainy days. It is often encountered prowling in wet meadows, and it is not averse to brackish pools of water.

The striped mud turtle appears to be mainly a scavenger, feeding upon all sorts of organic material. They have been observed raiding garbage piles in the vicinity of habitations and are readily caught on hooks baited with worms. No doubt on their journeys over the marshy grasslands they are searching for insects. In some sections of Florida they are known as "cow-dung turtles" from their habit of eating manure in pastures close by some weedy pond.

As a rule this is a docile and well-behaved turtle, much

less likely to bite than many of its group. In a terrarium it is not given to sulking at the bottom of its water dish, like the common mud turtle.

Figure 7.   Yellow mud turtle.

YELLOW MUD TURTLE

Kinosternon flavescens (Agassiz)

This is a mud turtle of the western states occupying a wide range from southern Nebraska through Kansas and Oklahoma, and most of Texas, and on into Mexico. Its range extends westward to Utah and Arizona. Specimens occur in isolated sections of Illinois, but these are regarded by many authorities as a subspecies and are listed as *Kinosternon flavescens spooneri* Smith.

This is one of the largest of the mud turtles, examples more than five and one-half inches long being recorded. The carapace is short and broad, rather low, and oval in outline. It is flattened on top and sometimes even depressed along the median line, sort of dividing the shell into two sections. The surface is quite smooth. The plastron is moderately large and sturdy, capable of being closed partially.

The color is greenish brown above, the seams of each shield standing out as black lines. The plastron is yellowish, its seams rather broad, and the fleshy parts of this species are dusky above and paler below. The throat and sides of the neck often show yellowish blotches.

This is also a turtle of small ponds, rarely found in rivers or streams. It, too, forages on land during rainy weather and is likely to migrate from one pond to another during the dry season. Its food consists chiefly of worms, small mollusks, and crustaceans and insects.

SNAPPING TURTLE

Chelydra serpentina (Linne)

The common snapping turtle is at home over most of the country east of the Rockies, from Canada to Mexico. Its place in peninsular Florida is taken by a slightly different subspecies. Throughout most of this wide geographic range this is the largest, and certainly the meanest, species of turtle to be found.

Figure 8.   Snapping turtle.

A large specimen measures about fourteen inches in shell-length and may weigh from thirty to forty pounds. Numerous fifty-pound snappers have been recorded, and a few that have hit the seventy-pound mark. The carapace is oval, not highly arched, and has several deep notches in its rear margin. There are three blunt, broken keels on the back, rough and conspicuous in young individuals, but likely to be worn and smoothed in old specimens. The plastron is small and somewhat crosslike in form, and it gives very little protection to the reptile's fleshy parts. The bridges between the two parts of the shell are very narrow. The body of this turtle can best be described as bulky. It generally appears too big for its shell and seems to bulge in all directions. The head is large and the neck is long and rubbery, but the creature is capable of withdrawing the whole thing completely into its shell. The eyes are set well forward and well up toward the top of the head. The limbs are massive, the feet bearing rugged claws. The tail is long and stout with a row of enlarged horny shields along its upper edge. The beak is very strongly hooked, and there are usually two short barbels on the animal's chin. Numerous wartlike tubercles are present on the limbs and the neck.

Snapping turtles are present in most of our lakes, larger ponds, and rivers and are usually more plentiful than one would suspect, since they are rarely seen at the surface. They do not crawl out on objects to bask in the sun and seldom leave the water at all, except to come ashore in July for the purpose of laying eggs. During dry seasons they will migrate overland if their pond dries up. They are far from helpless or even awkward on land, however, and travel with rugged determination and fair speed for such lumbering creatures. A half-grown specimen will climb over a one-foot wire fence that would safely confine most turtles or tortoises.

The snapping turtle is a savage, cross-tempered brute, largely carnivorous. A good share of its time is spent half-buried in the mud, where it looks for all the world like a mossy boulder. When a fish swims by, the head darts out with incredible speed, and there is one less fish in that particular pond. This turtle can strike with the rapidity and precision of a rattlesnake. Fish, however, are not the only victims. It eagerly devours frogs and young muskrats and is very destructive to waterfowl, especially young ducks. Even adult ducks are grabbed from below and dragged down to be torn apart and consumed on the pond's bottom.

In spite of these known facts, the record of the snapping turtle is not as bad as some would have us believe. Careful examination of the stomach contents from large series of snappers in the wild indicate that attacks on birds or mammals are very scarce, and that game fish constitute only a small portion of their total food. Surprisingly enough, a considerable amount of vegetable matter is consumed, along with snails, crustaceans, and insects. The relatively small number of game fish and pan fish in its diet would be further reduced when you consider that many of them were undoubtedly found dead, as the snapper is a great consumer of carrion. Those charged with the responsibility of maintaining waterfowl breeding areas or fish hatcheries have to take precautions and usually spare no effort to rid their waters of snapping turtles, but the wholesale slaughter of them in open ponds and lakes, in the name of conservation, is a tragic mistake.

Late in June or early in July the female snapping turtle comes ashore looking for a suitable spot to deposit her eggs. She may travel a hundred yards or more from the water before she finds just what she wants, a section of loose damp soil at the edge of some wooded area. Here she digs a hole, using only her hind legs, and deposits from twenty to forty eggs that are white, brittle shelled, and spherical in shape. The author once observed such a laying and, after the turtle had crudely covered her nest and departed, took the thirty-three round eggs home and put them in a box of dirt. This was on June 24. They were sprinkled lightly with water every four or five days, and they hatched on September 3, a total of 71 days. Despite the snapping turtle's usual habit of going some little distance inland for egg laying, it has been known to excavate its nest on the top of a muskrat house, right smack in the pond itself.

Figure 9. Eggs of snapping turtle.

The snapping turtle has long been known as a succulent table delicacy, and it is big enough so that one example provides a considerable amount of meat. The famed New England "turtle soup" was usually made of this species, and according to Babcock in *Turtles of New England* (1919) it used to be a common custom to keep a snapping turtle in the swill barrel, where it grew exceedingly fat and tender. He reports one individual attaining the weight of eighty-six pounds!

Snapping turtles had best not be handled. When on the ground their whole body lunges forward with each strike of the head, so that the reptile actually jumps at you. They can strike sideways as well as back over the shell (nearly half-way back), and a fair-sized specimen with its knifelike jaws can inflict a serious wound. Furthermore, once they secure a grip they hang on with the tenacity of a bulldog, and you can even behead the creatures without loosening their hold in the slightest. The only safe way to carry a specimen is by the tail, holding him well away from your body.

ALLIGATOR SNAPPING TURTLE

Macrochelys temmincki (Troost)

This awesome creature resembles a huge, overgrown snapping turtle and is the largest fresh-water turtle found in this country. It lives in the rivers flowing into the Gulf

Figure 10. Alligator snapping turtle.

of Mexico, from Texas to western Florida. Its center of abundance is in the lower Mississippi Valley, where it ranges north as far as central Illinois.

The carapace is very rough, moderately arched, and has three prominent tuberculated ridges running lengthwise, present even in old adults. The outline is oval, the anterior margin smooth, and the posterior margin deeply serrate. The plastron is almost ludicrously small. The head is tremendously large, pointed, and its top is covered with plates instead of skin, as in the common snapping turtle. The eyes are placed at the sides of the head, not toward the top. The shell is brownish black in color but is invariably coated with a bristly growth of algae. The soft parts are dark brown above, lighter underneath. The alligator snapping turtle attains a maximum length of about twenty-eight inches and a weight of nearly 150 pounds. Even larger specimens have been reported, including a veritable giant of 403 pounds from Kansas, but any record over 150 pounds needs verification.

This reptile is undisputed monarch of all it surveys and is as savage and vicious as it looks, although it is probably not as dangerous as the common snapping turtle. The explanation for this is that the alligator snapping turtle is far more sluggish; and it lacks the long, flexible neck that gives the common snapper such an advantage in offensive maneuvering. When annoyed, the alligator snapping turtle simply sits there with its mouth opened widely, and it rarely bites unless the object of its annoyance is only inches away. One can pick up a specimen quite safely by grasping the shell just above the neck, with the other hand supporting the rear margin. The reptile is unable to twist its neck enough to reach your hand, but it should be emphasized that this is *not* a safe way to handle the common snapping turtle.

This species has a small, pink, wormlike appendage inside of its mouth, well back on the tongue; and it is able to keep this filament in motion, giving it the appearance of a live grub. Undoubtedly many an unwary fish is enticed to within grabbing range by this lure. It is interesting to know that where this turtle inhabits the tributaries of larger rivers, it commonly migrates upstream at a rate of three or four miles a year; and it has been suggested that fishes in a single area soon learn not to be fooled by this attractive worm in murky waters, and the turtle has to move on to new locations in order to find uneducated fish. Besides fish, the alligator snapping turtle eats frogs, crustaceans, mollusks, and some vegetable material. Not being as aggressive as the common snapping turtle, it probably seldom bothers birds or mammals, although it will eat any dead animal that sinks to the bottom.

One good look at this creature's massive head and jaws leaves no doubt as to its dangerous possibilities, but at the same time its strength has often been exaggerated. One sometimes sees the statement that it can bite completely through a broom handle or an axe handle, but in reality it is nowhere near that powerful. However, it is obvious that one should exercise extreme caution whenever handling an angered specimen.

While we cannot exactly call such an animal "timid," it is very retiring in its habits, and largely nocturnal, so that in spite of its being far from rare, it is not very often observed. For several years it was merely regarded as an extra large snapping turtle, but it may be differentiated from the common snapper (which shares parts of its range) by the following characteristics, in addition to its much greater dimensions.

Alligator Snapping Turtle	*Common Snapping Turtle*
Three distinct keels on back	Keels obscure on back
Head triangular, covered with plates	Head oval, covered with closely adherent skin
Upper mandible with fossette for tooth of lower mandible	No fossette for tooth of lower mandible
Marginal plates 31, with double series at sides	Marginal plates 25, with single series at sides
Tail round, covered with 3 rows of circular plates	Tail more or less oval, surmounted with a crest of wedge-shaped plates.

SPOTTED TURTLE

Clemmys guttata (Schneider)

The little spotted turtle, commonly miscalled a "mud turtle," is an inhabitant of marshy places from Maine to central Michigan and northern Illinois. Its range extends south as far as eastern Georgia, and possibly to northern Florida.

A really big example is about five inches long. The shell is ovoid and moderately elevated, with the top more or less flattish. The surface is generally smooth, particularly with mature individuals, with the edges evenly rounded. The

Figure 11.   Spotted turtle.

plastron is large and oval. The color is dull black, with irregularly spaced yellow dots, and occasionally a few orange spots. The dots vary considerably both in number and in position, but are always present. Usually there is one yellow dot in each marginal shield and from three to five on each of the costal and vertebral shields. The plastron is yellow in the center with heavy blotches of black around the edges, with some specimens having a plastron that is nearly solid black.

The upper surface of the head, neck, and limbs is black, sometimes with a few yellow spots, especially on the neck; and back of the eye is a conspicuous orange-yellow patch. This patch is larger and more accentuated in females, who generally have bright orange eyes, while those of the male are brown. Underneath, the fleshy parts are salmon-pink. The tail is much longer in the male than it is in the female.

This little turtle is at home in swamps, marshes, and the boggy portions of small ponds but does not often venture into the larger lakes and has no use at all for the rollicking tempo of a river which may rush along at a mile or two an hour. An ideal spot to look for specimens is where a small brook meanders through low meadows, here and there spreading out to form grassy pools. This species is nearly as fond of sunning itself as the painted turtle but does not associate itself with others of its kind so commonly, and usually only one, or at most two, are to be seen on the same log or rock. Perhaps its favorite sunning spot is in the center of some clump of water grass, surrounded by shallow water. Sometimes one finds miniature islands of bunch grass that are matted down by the turtles that go there regularly for their sun bath. When approached, they slide off their perch and frantically endeavor to get out of sight beneath the ferns and grasses of their watery home.

The spotted turtle eats just about what one would expect of an animal so partial to marshy situations. The major part of its diet consists of insects and their larvae, supplemented by worms, crustaceans, small mollusks, and occasionally tadpoles. Frogs and fish are sometimes eaten, but probably in most cases these vertebrates are found dead. Captive specimens will eat lettuce, so it is probable that it feeds upon various water plants in the wild to some extent, but it is chiefly a carnivorous reptile. It appears to be unable to swallow unless its head is completely submerged.

The eggs are laid in June and are generally very few in number. Very often a single egg is deposited, with three

making up the average "clutch." The female scoops out
a shallow excavation in loose, dry soil, usually on some hillside close by the marsh; and the little turtles hatch about
the middle of September, at least in Connecticut. The
youngsters are just about an inch long at hatching and almost as wide, so that their shells are nearly circular. At this
stage they usually have one spot on each shield but get
more with advancing age.

We might call this species the small boys' favorite, as it is
easily captured, does well in captivity (if provided with a
small puddle of water), and is quite strikingly marked for a
turtle. Furthermore, it is entirely inoffensive and no amount
of teasing can induce it to bite. It is too small to have any
value as food for man, and it certainly is no menace to any
other form of life that might be considered as economically
beneficial. It takes only a few days for the spotted turtle
to get over its habit of withdrawing into its shell every time
you look at it, and most individuals soon become quite tame.

MUHLENBERG'S TURTLE

Clemmys muhlenbergi (Schoepff)

Muhlenberg's turtle is a small species, not more than four
inches and generally averaging about three and one-half
inches long. It has a rather restricted range, being found
from western Pennsylvania through southern and central
New York to southern New England. Toward the south, it
occurs to western North Carolina. The distribution is not
continuous over this area; and the species is rare in some
sections, relatively common in others, and apparently absent
in still others. It is generally less common in the eastern
parts of its range.

The shell is oval and slightly elongate, the sides frequently somewhat parallel; it is moderately arched, sometimes showing a feeble keel, particularly with young examples. The concentric rings of each shield of the carapace
are rather deeply impressed, so that this species lacks the

Figure 12.   Muhlenberg's turtle.

smooth shell of the spotted turtle just discussed. The plastron is large and deeply notched at the rear. The color is dark brown or black, with faint yellowish or reddish patches at the center of each shield. There may be yellowish splashes, but this species never exhibits the neat round dots so characteristic of its relative, the spotted turtle. The plastron is black, irregularly blotched with yellow. The head and limbs are black above and pinkish below, the upper surface more or less mottled with yellow. There is a large patch of bright orange on each side of the head, well back of the eye.

Muhlenberg's turtle feeds upon worms, snails, crustaceans, and probably any dead fish or frog it may chance upon. Insects and berries have been found in the stomachs of dissected specimens, so this species is probably somewhat omnivorous in the wild state. It does not need to be underwater in order to eat but does just about as well on dry land.

The breeding habits are about the same as those of the spotted turtle. Very few eggs are laid, and these are deposited in a hole excavated by the female in June. In general habits and choice of living quarters it closely resembles the spotted turtle, and sometimes the two are somewhat alike in color as well. However, the species can always be identified by the conspicuous orange patches back of its eyes. It is a very gentle turtle, never entertaining any notions about biting, and makes a fine pet. It was named in honor of Reverend Henry Muhlenberg of Pennsylvania, an early American naturalist who sent the first specimen to Mr. Schoepff to be described, back in 1801.

PACIFIC POND TURTLE

Clemmys marmorata (Baird and Girard)

This is the only fresh-water turtle to be found along the Pacific coast, from southwestern British Columbia to the San Francisco Bay area of California. A subspecies (*pallida*) occurs from there to Baja California, and in the San Francisco Bay region the two forms intergrade.

This is a rather dull-hued turtle, its shell low and oval, a little wider at the posterior half. The plastron is large, well protecting the underside, with a weak notch at the rear. The length is from five to seven inches. The color of the carapace varies from dark olive to almost black, with or without mottling; but commonly there is a feeble pattern of forking lines on each shield, paler in tone than the ground color. The plastron is yellow, with irregular black smudges along the lines that separate the shields. The surface is nearly smooth in mature specimens, but with youngsters there may be a slight keel. The head and neck are dark olive above, the sides of the neck are generally mottled with darker spots, and the chin and throat are yellow. The limbs and tail may be dark with paler clouding or yellowish brown with darker clouding.

This is a thoroughly aquatic turtle, apparently venturing out on dry land only for the purpose of egg laying. It occurs in ponds and lakes and in streams, sometimes frequents brackish waters, and on occasion has been known to enter the sea. It is perhaps predominantly a turtle of quiet, muddy waters; but well up in the mountain areas it has been found living in clear, swift-moving streams. It is an extremely wary creature, taking alarm at the first evidence of danger; and it is not an easy turtle to catch.

This being the only turtle found along the West Coast, it has been intensively trapped for the market despite its relatively small size. A generation or two ago it brought as much as six dollars a dozen in the trade. Back in the last century a writer declared that this turtle, once so abundant in the San Francisco region, was now (1879) very scarce owing to the commercial trappers.

WOOD TURTLE

Clemmys insculpta (LeConte)

The wood turtle occurs from Nova Scotia all through New England and south through Pennsylvania to about central Virginia. From New York State it ranges west through Ontario and across Michigan and Wisconsin to eastern Iowa, but it appears to be absent in Ohio, Indiana, and Illinois.

The length is about eight inches, and the carapace is oval, not highly arched, and strongly keeled. It is serrate at the rear margin, where it flares slightly upward. Each dorsal shield is sculptured with many concentric ridges, rising to a sort of blunt pyramid, its apex closer to the rear. The plastron is heavy and deeply notched at the back. The limbs are sturdy, the head moderately large, with the upper jaw notched at its tip. The feet are partially webbed, the hind toes more so than those up front.

The color of the carapace is dull brown, tinged with reddish, often with obscure yellowish marks. Young specimens sometimes exhibit narrow yellow lines radiating from the summit of each dorsal shield. The plastron is yellow, and each of its shields contains a large black spot at its outer margin, and more black spots are present on the under side

Figure 13. The wood turtle rights itself.

of the marginal shields back of the bridge. The animal's head and limbs are dark brown above and brick-red underneath.

This is the least aquatic member of its genus, being almost as terrestrial as the box turtle during most of the summer. It will be found in moist woods and timbered swamps and also in open woods and brushy fields. It is a good swimmer, and in the spring is often seen in brooks, and again in the late fall it returns to a watery home to spend the winter buried in the soft mud, commonly in an old muskrat burrow. From May to October, the wood turtle prefers to prowl overland through the forests and open grasslands, often miles from any water.

In food habits this species is omnivorous, although it shows a certain preference for vegetable food, especially berries. Heavily stained beaks and forefeet leave no ques-

tion as to its principal food during the blueberry season.
Strawberries are another favorite item, along with the leaves
and tender parts of a great many plants of forest and field.
To this strictly vegetarian diet is added insects and their
larvae, and any small creatures such as salamanders and
earthworms that are slow enough to be caught and small
enough to be overpowered. Captive specimens do very
nicely on a diet of lettuce, supplemented by an occasional
worm or caterpillar; and if you want to tempt a jaded appetite try offering a couple of ripe strawberries.

The wood turtle is easily tamed and is probably the most
satisfactory of all our turtles to keep as a pet. It is a hardy
species, easy to keep well fed, and shows more intelligence
than one would expect from a member of the reptile clan.
They soon learn to come to you and take food from your
hand and will even "beg" for food like a dog at times. Several writers have noted this action in which the turtle ap-
proaches, stretches its neck out full length, and stands as tall
as it can on three legs, while it holds one foreleg in the air.
Tinklepaugh, in 1932, experimented with wood turtles in a
maze and reached the conclusion that their ability to learn
the correct route to food was about equal to that of a rat.
This species is about as good natured as a turtle can be and
never seems to mind how much it is handled. However, it
is just as well to remember that a turtle of this size is capable
of giving one a nip that is painful; so it is wise to use ordinary caution in handling even this mild-mannered fellow, as
occasionally an individual will bite, although such action is
quite rare.

The eggs, numbering anywhere from four to twelve, are
laid early in June, the female excavating a hole in the soil,
commonly near a stump at the edge of the woods. The eggs
are nearly an inch and a half long, white, and have thin
shells. Hatching takes place in September. Unlike the more
aquatic turtles that usually nest close to the water, nests of
this species are not often discovered; and very young wood
turtles are seldom seen.

This turtle is not eaten to any extent these days, although

it is said to be excellent for that purpose. In fact, in the past it was commonly sold in the markets throughout its range and was hunted so persistently that at one time the state of New York passed a law protecting the wood turtle from capture for sale in the market. Today it is one of the commonest and best known of any of our turtles.

BLANDING'S TURTLE

Emys blandingi (Holbrook)

Blanding's turtle, sometimes known as the "semibox turtle," might be described as a cool-climate reptile. It is rather common in our North Central states such as Ohio, Illinois, and Indiana, but only in the central and northern regions, being absent from their southern portions. It ranges as far west as eastern Nebraska and occurs as far east as southern New England. It does not live near the coast and appears to be most abundant in Ohio and Indiana.

This is a fairly large turtle, averaging between seven and eight inches in length. The record is a little over nine inches. The shell is long and relatively narrow—much less round than the box turtle—and is moderately well arched, its top flattened a little. The plastron is large, notched at the back, and has a well-developed hinge between the pectoral and abdominal shields, the forward half functioning fairly well but the rear half closing only part way. The feet are broadly webbed, the neck is long, and the head sturdy. This species lacks the hooked beak of the box turtle.

The color is black, with each shield pretty well covered with pale yellow spots and sometimes scrawls. The plastron is yellow with large, irregular, black patches along both sides. The head and limbs are dark above, speckled or mottled with yellow; but the chin and throat are bright, immaculate yellow.

One usually thinks of Blanding's turtle as a land animal, but in reality it is far more aquatic than is generally be-

Figure 14. Blanding's turtle.

lieved. Its feet are strongly webbed, it is a fine swimmer, and it is well equipped for life in the water. Nearly one hundred individuals were taken in turtle traps set in Lake Michigan in 1937. Perhaps its favorite haunts would be in low-lying, swampy country, and in wet, grassy meadows separating small ponds or streams. It is not likely to be found in large lakes but often occurs in the weedy coves of such places, as witness the Lake Michigan record cited above.

The semibox turtle accepts a variety of food but is chiefly carnivorous. Some vegetable and plant material is eaten; but if the specimen is living near the water, and most of them are, its food consists chiefly of crustaceans and insects. Fish, mollusks, worms, and carrion are taken when the opportunity offers; and the turtle eats with equal ability upon the ground or underwater.

During the winter months Blanding's turtle hibernates in the mud at the bottom of some pond. It doesn't seem to mind the cold too much and often comes out of hibernation in February, while the weather is still plenty frigid in the northern states. Specimens have been observed swimming under the ice in January. At this season they are fully aquatic, for of course they would not be able to find any food on land until later in the spring. As a matter of fact, they probably eat very little at this time of year, for turtles can go a long time without food when they have to.

Blanding's turtle is a timid creature. If discovered at the edge of a pond it will plop into the water, swim to the bottom, wriggle into the soft mud, and stay there until it is sure the coast is clear again. If surprised on land it will stay in its shell for hours at a time, just so long as it thinks there is danger afoot. It cannot close its shell completely like the box turtle can, but its partially closing plastron does afford it a considerable measure of protection.

This is a very mild-mannered reptile, never making any attempt to bite. It makes an excellent species to keep for a pet, and specimens have lived for years in zoos. It is generally not particularly abundant throughout most of its range, and in the east it could be classed as rather uncommon. In captivity it does not require a tank but will live contentedly in a dry cage, of course with an ample supply of drinking water.

BOX TURTLE

Terrapene carolina (Linne)

The common box turtle, or box tortoise, is a familiar creature to those who go on berrying trips, or for any reason tramp over sunny hillsides and across brushy pastures during the summer months. This species occurs in the eastern states from Maine to Georgia and Alabama and west to the Mississippi River. Three subspecies extend its range well into Texas, along the Gulf Coast, and to Florida, while a closely related species occupies a wide range in the prairie country west of the Mississippi.

The box turtle averages between five and six inches in length. The upper shell is highly domed and almost globular, being only slightly longer than it is wide, with a blunt but distinct keel running down the center. The front and rear margins curl upward, giving the carapace somewhat the outlines of an old German military helmet. The plastron is hinged near the middle, dividing it into two movable lobes, so that it can be drawn up tightly against the upper shell.

The first thing one notices when he picks up a box turtle is this ability of the reptile to shut itself completely away from the world, making an impregnable fortress of its shelly covering. The lower shell, with its flexible hinge near the middle, is movable fore and aft. Hence, after drawing in his head and limbs, these two movable parts fold up against the upper shell; and Mr. Box Turtle is sealed in a tightly fitting suit of armor that is probably proof against all of its enemies except man. So tightly do the shells fit together that it is impossible to force a sheet of paper between them.

The colors of this turtle are fairly constant, but the markings are extremely variable; in fact, it is not often that one can find two individuals that are marked alike. The carapace is dark brown, decorated with numerous irregular, elongate, yellowish marks. These are usually arranged in more or less definite star-shaped clusters, one to a shield. On half-grown

Figure 15.   Box turtle.

youngsters the markings may be deep yellow or even orange.
The plastron may be uniformly yellowish brown or there
may be blotches of brown or black. The central portion is
commonly dark, with the paler areas at the sides. The neck
and limbs are usually well mottled with yellow and brown.
The eyes of the male are bright red, while those of the female

are dark brown in color. This turtle has but four toes on each hind foot, and its beak is strongly hooked.

The box turtle is mainly terrestrial, although it will be found in more or less swampy or marshy country. They are fair swimmers and occasionally are seen in both fresh-water ponds and salty lagoons; but for the most part they are at home in open grassy woodlands, pastures and meadows, and sunny hillside thickets. They are confirmed wanderers and don't believe in staying in one locality as most turtles do. Marked individuals have been retaken a week later as much as a mile from the place of their release. In mountainous country they are known to occur at an elevation of several thousand feet. Unlike the gopher tortoise of the South, this species does not burrow, although it may take refuge in an abandoned woodchuck burrow during excessively hot weather.

During hot and dry periods, however, the box turtle often seeks some drying-out mud hole in the woods and partially buries itself in the deep oozy mire, sometimes several specimens being found so buried in the mud bordering a single pool. This may be a sort of estivation, for they remain immovable for days, until a drought-breaking rain sends them tramping back to the fields and meadows.

The box turtle is an omnivorous feeder. When young it is apt to stay pretty close to marshes and other moist situations; and its food is largely animal, such things as worms, mollusks, insect larvae, and crustaceans. The adults seem to prefer fruits and berries, mushrooms, and tender grasses and leaves; although they will accept worms, snails, slugs, and similar animal matter. Their fondness for fungi is well known, and there are several cases on record where people have been made sick after eating a box turtle that had apparently been feeding on poisonous toadstools that seemed to have no ill effects on the turtle at all. Occasionally an individual wanders into a garden and wreaks havoc on the tender lettuce or bites chunks out of squashes or melons. Captive specimens will eat fruits and berries of many kinds and are especially fond of overripe bananas.

A rather comical situation sometimes develops when food is plentiful, as at the height of the wild strawberry season. Some box turtles get so fat that they cannot close their shells completely, and when the forward section is forced shut the rear end of the turtle is squeezed out at the back, and when that lobe is tightly closed the turtle's head and forelimbs are forced out at the front.

Box turtles are invariably timid creatures and may be kept as pets without any fear of bites. When first captured they show a reluctance to leave the protection of their armor and may remain tightly closed up for an hour or more. However, they eventually screw up enough courage to venture a look around and in due time become very tame. They are rather more intelligent than the strictly aquatic turtles and can be taught to beg for food and to take it from your fingers.

Egg laying takes place in June or July in the more northern parts of its range and is generally accomplished late in the afternoon or in the evening. The female excavates a shallow, flask-shaped nest, working exclusively with her hind feet. The site selected is in loose soil as a rule but may even be in the turf of some well-kept lawn. The eggs usually number four or five and are elliptical in shape, a little more than an inch long, and are white and brittle shelled. Hatching takes place in the fall, and the little turtles go into hibernation soon after. It is believed that they do not eat anything until the following spring. Very young box turtles are among the rarest of Nature's children, and it is extremely unusual to encounter one in the field.

It is probable that newly hatched or very young box turtles are preyed upon by skunks and other carnivores, and to some extent by snakes; and crows have been known to devour them. But once they get to be three or four inches long they are practically immune from danger, owing to the powerful muscles which close the plastron so tightly that no predaceous animal is able to tear the shell apart. Their greatest enemy is the forest fire, and of course man. If they can avoid accidents—and many are killed annually on our highways—box turtles live to a ripe old age and may very well represent the oldest living animals in this country. There are numerous instances of thirty and forty years recorded in captivity, and at least one case of a venerable old fellow sixty-six years old and still feeling hale and hearty. The works of Nichols and Fowler, who have carefully evaluated the abundant reports of great age attained by box turtles, suggest that they may reach an age somewhat over one hundred years.

The Florida box turtle, *Terrapene carolina bauri* Taylor, is a subspecies occupying peninsular Florida and intergrading to some extent with the typical form in the northern part of that state. It differs from the common box turtle in the following ways: the shell is more elongate, with its highest

Figure 16.   Florida box turtle.

part well back from the middle of the shell, over the rump. The markings on the carapace lean more to long, unbroken radiating lines of bright yellow in place of the starlike clusters of spots. There are usually two well-defined yellowish

lines on the side of the head, and in most cases there are
but three toes on each hind foot.

   Terrapene carolina major (Agassiz) occurs along the Gulf
Coast from Texas to the Florida panhandle. It is a large
form, seven inches or more long, with a well-domed shell
that is highest in the center. It is the largest of the box
turtles of this country. The color is dark brown and is sometimes without markings of any kind, but usually there are
weak radiating streaks not unlike those of *bauri*. The plastron is generally black. In this subspecies the hind foot has
four toes.

Figure 17.   Three-toed box turtle.

   The so-called three-toed box turtle, *Terrapene carolina
triunguis* (Agassiz), is not well named, since *bauri* from
Florida also has but three toes on its hind feet in many instances. However, this subspecies has a narrow shell that is
well arched, well keeled, and flaring a little at the rear
margin. The carapace is brown with irregular yellowish
scrawls, with the plastron solid black as a rule. The head
and limbs, especially the forelimbs, are heavily spotted with

brown and yellow. This subspecies may be found chiefly west of the Mississippi River, from Texas north through Colorado to northern Missouri. It occurs also east of the river in Alabama and Mississippi. It is sometimes known as the midland box turtle. The general habits of these three subspecies are substantially the same as those of the typical form.

WESTERN BOX TURTLE

Terrapene ornata (Agassiz)

This is a terrestrial turtle of the western plains, at home from South Dakota through Wyoming to Texas, Arizona, and New Mexico. It gets as far eastward as northern Indiana but south of Illinois is not found east of the Mississippi River.

The carapace is oval and broad, its length nearly six inches. The shell is arched, but it is rather flat on top, and it lacks the dorsal keel so characteristic of the eastern box turtles of the *carolina* group. The color is dark brown, with numerous bars of yellow radiating from a broken central line. The plastron is almost black, with a pattern of yellow lines running in all directions. This oddly marked lower shell, plus the absence of a keel on the upper shell, easily distinguishes this species from the common box turtle of the East. The head and neck of this species, and its limbs, are generally well speckled with pale yellow.

The Western box turtle, also called the ornate box turtle, is essentially a prairie species and can more easily stand drier situations than its eastern cousin. In the eastern parts of its range it is most abundant in sand dune country, while in the Southwest it shows a great deal of tolerance for semi-arid conditions. It is not often seen in wooded areas and almost never enters the water.

This is another mild-mannered turtle which may be handled safely from the start. Always remember, however, that any species, no matter how gentle, will occasionally

Figure 18. Western box turtles, and two views of a rattle used by the
Plains Indians.

produce an ornery individual that may nip your finger. Like
the other box turtles, this one tames easily and does very well
as a pet, feeding contentedly on lettuce, berries and other
fruits, grasshoppers and worms, and even bits of raw meat.

The ornate box turtle appears to go into hibernation earlier than the common one of the East, and it is later in the spring when they appear again. During the hot months of summer they are likely to be inactive during the day, often hiding away in some abandoned rodent burrow, and coming out just before dusk to roam about. A rainy day at this season can be depended upon to bring them out in numbers.

The Plains Indians used to make rattles of their shells by boiling out the fleshy parts of the turtle and then fastening the plastron tight up against the carapace, after inserting a few rounded pebbles. The shell was then decorated with feathers and bits of leather, sometimes provided with a handle, and was ready for ceremonial use. It is interesting to note that other tribes did the same thing with whatever species of turtle that happened to be at hand. Examples are known from the Seminoles of Florida, the Iroquois of New York, and many others; but the tightly fitting shells of the box turtles seem to be the best fitted for this purpose.

DIAMONDBACK TERRAPIN

Malaclemys terrapin (Schoepff)

This is the celebrated turtle that plays the leading role in that famous culinary production, "Terrapin Stew." Several of our larger pond turtles are excellent eating, and many of them succeed in getting into the markets labelled as "terrapin," but the diamondback is in a class by itself as a highly prized delicacy. Six-inch specimens used to sell for as much as seventy dollars a dozen. A salt-marsh turtle, its range is from Massachusetts to Florida and west to Texas. Six subspecies are recognized throughout this area.

The turtle we will consider first is the typical one of the species, listed properly as *Malaclemys terrapin terrapin* (Schoepff), which occurs from Cape Cod in Massachusetts to Cape Hatteras in North Carolina. Perhaps it would be more accurate to say it used to enjoy this range, for it is currently quite rare or totally absent over much of this area.

Figure 19.   Diamondback terrapin.

The average size of this northern form is five or six inches in length, and about eight inches is the probable maximum. The female is noticeably larger than the male. The shell is low, broad, and rough. It is nearly oval in outline but is slightly wedge-shaped, with its widest point somewhat back of the middle. The top of the carapace is usually without a dorsal keel; if present, it is low and inconspicuous and is not tuberculated, a point of difference between this turtle and the subspecies from the Gulf of Mexico. Each shield of the carapace is deeply sculptured with angular grooves, the shield depressed at its center. The plastron is long and nar-row, the bridge rather short.

The head and neck are comparatively small, smaller in proportion to the shell than is the case of the more southern forms. The limbs are sturdy, all four feet being strongly webbed. The color of the fleshy parts is some shade of gray, occasionally greenish gray but usually simply pale gray; and the legs and neck are not striped but are heavily dotted with black. The carapace is generally brown, sometimes almost blackish; and the concentric lines of sculpture on each shield are darker in hue. The plastron may be yellowish gray or

almost orange, often with darker markings. As with many
of our turtles, the most sharply defined markings and the
brightest colors are to be seen on young, partly grown individuals.

This turtle is at home in brackish waters and is never
found away from the coast. Its ideal environment is some
extensive salt marsh, where it can swim about in the deeper
tidal creeks and wander over the mud flats while the tides
are out. It is found, too, on open sea coasts where muddy
and grassy conditions exist; and it is known to occur well up
in tidal rivers and estuaries, but its principal locale is the
salty grass and mud areas just back from the open coast line.

The diamondback feeds upon fish, that it may find dead,
and on marine worms, fiddler crabs, and various small mollusks; in fact, it will probably eat any crustacean or shellfish
that it can crush. The common periwinkle, so abundant in
the marshes, has been listed as a food item; but it is doubt-
ful if the turtle's jaws are powerful enough to crush the
shells of these rugged snails. At commercial establishments
where attempts have been made to rear terrapins for the
market, they are fed chiefly with fish and crabs, cut into
small pieces and scattered on the ground near their tanks.
The turtles crawl out and take the food, returning to the
water to swallow it.

Egg laying begins about the middle of May in the Chesapeake Bay region and early in June in southern New England. The eggs are buried in sandy soil well above the high-
tide mark in an excavation made by the female with her
hind legs. The number may be anywhere between five and
twelve, and they hatch in about three months.

Back in the "Gay Nineties," the diamondback suddenly
became very popular as a special delicacy and the demand
from metropolitan hotels and restaurants was so great that
almost fabulous prices were offered for them. At first only
the northern form, *terrapin*, brought top prices, and they
were called "Chesapeakes" in the trade because most of the
turtles were supplied from the Chesapeake Bay region.
Southern forms were commonly shipped to certain points on

the bay to be reshipped to the larger cities as "Chesapeakes." The author does not know if one subspecies excels another in flavor. The difference certainly cannot be great, however, or Chesapeake dealers would not, for many years, have been able to sell southern turtles as "Chesapeakes." In 1891 the total shipped from this area was estimated at 89,150 pounds.

The demand for terrapins eventually exceeded production, for the creatures could not stand the heavy drain. They do not reproduce rapidly, and growth is gained slowly. Probably the greatest single factor in the decline of this reptile was the indiscriminate taking of anything even closely resembling an adult. Specimens only four inches long were eagerly trapped, long before they had reached breeding age, and before too many years there were precious few mature turtles left to carry on the race. Some system of conservation might have resulted in a steady supply of diamondbacks, but at this date it is an unusual experience to run across a specimen in the wild. In the last decade or two the popularity of terrapin stew has declined almost to the vanishing point. The turtles are no longer trapped for the market, and it is encouraging to note that the species appears to be making a comeback in many localities throughout its long range.

It was evident by the beginning of the present century that these valuable reptiles seemed doomed to extinction, and in 1902 the United States Fish Commission instituted a program at Chesapeake Bay to study the diamondback terrapin and to determine its adaptability to artificial propagation. At a result of this study, and others of the same nature by the states involved, several commercial "turtle farms" have been established with varying success; and there is probably more information available on the biology and the habits of this species than on any other American turtle. Some interesting observations from this experimental work follow:

Egg production fluctuates from five to twenty-nine during a single season, for a single female. Young turtles measure about one inch at hatching. They do not eat for a month or so and in the wild state go into hibernation while fasting, taking their first food the following spring. By keeping them in warm pens and feeding them during the winter, they gain about one year's growth over those that hibernate. Females attain a length of five inches and sexual maturity in five years. Males seldom exceed four and one-half inches. Growth, with winter feeding, is moderately rapid for about six years, followed by a much slower growth; and after an age of ten years its attained growth is so slow that it is almost negligible.

In its natural home, the diamondback hibernates in the muds of the salt marsh; and old-time epicures used to claim that the finest flavored terrapin were those dug from the mud in early spring.

The southern diamondback terrapin, *Malaclemys terrapin centrata* (Latreille), is found from the southeastern end of Florida to Cape Hatteras, where it undoubtedly intergrades with the northern *terrapin* just discussed. The shell is a little more oval—less wedge-shaped—with more parallel sides. The plastron is less squarish back of the bridge, the head is proportionally larger, and the fleshy parts are usually darker in color.

The Florida diamondback terrapin, subspecies *macrospilota* Hay, lives along the Gulf Coast of Florida. Its chief distinguishing character is a bright yellow or orange area in the center of each shield; and since the carapace is almost black, these irregular patches of color produce a striking effect.

The Mississippi diamondback, subspecies *pileata* (Wied), used to be accorded full specific rank. It occurs from western Florida to Louisiana and may be recognized by its strongly tuberculated central keel. At the tip of the Florida peninsula, the subspecies *rhizophorarum* Fowler is found. Its back is decorated with prominent dorsal keels, and the general outline of the shell is decidedly oblong. This turtle is known locally as the mangrove diamondback.

The last subspecies of this interesting turtle is *littoralis* Hay, the Texas diamondback. In Louisiana it probably in-

Figure 20.   Florida diamondback terrapin.

tergrades with *pileata,* and it may be found all along the
Texas coast to the Mexican border, and beyond. Like all of
the Gulf varieties, it has a tuberculated dorsal keel; but its
shell is more domed than the others. It also grows to a
somewhat larger size than the Atlantic terrapins but has always been regarded as inferior to them in flavor. All of
these subspecies have essentially the same habits, prefer the
same kinds of food, and choose similar muddy salt-water
marshes in which to take up residence. All have been hunted
and trapped relentlessly, but the southern varieties are much
more common today than the typical form that was once so
abundant in the vicinity of Chesapeake Bay.

BARBOUR'S SAWBACK TURTLE

Graptemys barbouri Carr and Marchand

This is a turtle of the Southeast, at home in creeks and
rivers in southwestern Georgia and the panhandle region of
northern Florida. It has a maximum length of a little better
than ten inches, the average specimen being between six and

eight. The males are noticeably smaller, seldom exceeding
five inches in length.

The shell is elongate-oval and only moderately elevated.
It tapers to the rear, so that its highest point is closer to the
front. The surface is smooth, with a more or less prominent
central keel that is tuberculate. Young specimens, more
rounded in outline, show this keel as two or three backward-
pointing, thornlike spikes. The marginal shields on the
posterior end of the carapace present a sawtooth arrange-

Figure 21.   Barbour's sawback turtle.

ment. The plastron is large, well protecting the turtle's
underside. The color varies from dull olive green to greenish black, with weak paler markings on the costal shields in
the form of incomplete circles. The plastron is yellowish.
In young specimens, each of the marginal shields bears a
heavy dark blotch on its lower side.

The head is dark above, usually with three broad areas
of yellow, one between the eyes and one on each temple.
Smaller lines of yellow extend down the neck, branching
and forking; and there are narrow yellow lines on the limbs
and tail, all on a dark greenish-black ground color.

This turtle is a lover of clear, running water, preferably with a rock bottom. It will seldom be found in ponds, canals, or other quiet waters, much preferring some creek or river in which to live. Furthermore, Sawbacks will congregate where the bottom suits them, and sometimes they will be almost completely absent where a stretch of the river has a sandy bottom. Like most of its tribe, it enjoys sunning itself and is a sociable fellow, generally basking on some stone or tree root in company with others of its kind. It is quite wary, however, and slips into the water at the slightest alarm.

This species was not discovered until 1942, when the first specimen was described by Carr and Marchand. Not too much is known about its feeding and breeding habits, except that it is believed to feed chiefly upon mollusks, both river clams and snails.

MAP TURTLE

Graptemys geographica (LeSueur)

The common map turtle ranges from Quebec south through western New England and New York to Virginia, while in the Middle West it may be collected from Arkansas and Oklahoma north to Wisconsin and Minnesota. It is particularly common in Illinois and Indiana and south through Tennessee. It is a large species, some of the females attaining a shell length of ten inches. The males are considerably smaller.

The carapace is rather flattish and flaring behind, with a slightly sawtooth edge at the rear. The plastron is large and strong. A blunt keel extends down the back, bisecting the vertebral shields, and this keel may be prominent and tuberculate in some individuals and low and inconspicuous in others. Young specimens bear a very strongly keeled upper shell. The head is unusually large and rugged, the limbs are sturdy, and the feet are strongly webbed.

The color is dull olive brown, and the upper surface is generally covered with an irregular pattern of thin greenish or yellowish lines. It is a sort of reticulate pattern and has given the creature the popular name of "map turtle." With

Figure 22. Map turtle.

some specimens, these markings are very indistinct; and with others they can be seen clearly only when the shell is wet. As is the case with many of the turtles, the pattern is most effectively displayed on partly grown examples. The lower side of each marginal shield is yellow, with a conspicuous central blotch of brown. The plastron is pale yellow, often with a pinkish cast, and with faint greenish smudges along the sides. The seams of the plastron may be bordered by a single dark line, although these are not discernible in large specimens. The head and neck are dark olive or greenish black, striped with longitudinal lines of yellow; and there is an elongate, somewhat triangular yellow spot behind each eye. The limbs and tail are also decorated with thin yellowish lines.

This is more of a river turtle than a pond turtle. It prefers large bodies of water but may be found in coves and relatively quiet backwaters of streams. It is an excellent swimmer and is thoroughly aquatic in habits, never wandering about on land except at egg laying time. It is very fond of basking in the sun during warm weather, and a group will often congregate on some sandy or grassy bank for that purpose; although they also climb out on stumps, logs, and stones to soak up the sun's rays. This is one of the first turtles to appear in the spring, after the ice has left our watercourses but the temperature is still pretty cold, and it is one of the last to go into hibernation for the winter. Specimens may sometimes be seen swimming under thin ice in the late fall.

The map turtle's large head has strong and powerful jaws. The peculiar structure of the broadened jaws render them especially adapted for crushing small mollusks, which make up a large part of their diet. Crayfish are also eaten; and probably some vegetable matter is taken occasionally, although this species is predominantly carnivorous. Food is always swallowed underwater. Despite its rather formidable jaws, the map turtle is a timid creature; and even freshly caught adults almost never make any attempts at biting.

They will sometimes hiss but are quick to draw their head and limbs out of sight and wait patiently for the danger to pass.

In late May or early June the females leave the water and go searching for a suitable place to lay their eggs. They prefer sandy hillsides or freshly plowed fields and sometimes travel considerable distances to find just what they want. The ten to fourteen elongate white eggs are deposited in a flask-shaped excavation and are carefully covered with earth. Hatching takes place in early September as a rule. Sometimes a late set of eggs will winter over, the little turtles hatching the following May or June.

FALSE MAP TURTLE

Graptemys pseudogeographica (Gray)

This is a fair-sized turtle, attaining a length of eight or nine inches when fully grown. It occurs in the northern and central parts of the Mississippi drainage area, ranging north to Minnesota and south as far as Arkansas and Oklahoma. It gets as far east as Indiana and as far west as central Nebraska. A subspecies continues the range down through Texas and Louisiana to the Gulf of Mexico.

The shell is oval, widening a little at the rear, where the marginal shields render that end noticeably sawtoothed. There is a rather high dorsal keel that is characterized by a series of moderately sharp nodes. Other than this knobby keel, the carapace is smooth and only slightly arched. The plastron is long, and notched at the rear end.

The shell is dull olive brown, with a variable pattern. Usually each shield has a brownish blotch that is surrounded by pale yellow circular markings; but these markings may be obscure, particularly with old individuals. The marginal shields each bear a rounded spot at the rear, both above and on the underside. The plastron is dull yellow, sometimes with a darkened pattern along the seams. The fleshy parts

are dark greenish black with yellowish stripes. The limbs
and tail are boldly striped, as are the neck and throat, while
just back of the eyes are two broad concentric patches that
often curve down under the eyes.

This is a turtle of lakes, rivers, and ponds; but it shows
a distaste for strong currents and is seldom to be found
where the waters are clear and the bottom rocky or sandy.
It likes an abundance of aquatic vegetation in which it can
hide and undoubtedly secures a large part of its food on
weedy bottoms. Hence, one looks for the false map turtle in
reedy coves, backwater sloughs, and still waters generally.

Throughout the Middle West it is one of the most abundant species of turtle and has long been a favorite for food.
Most epicures rate it as second only to the diamondback of
the Eastern seaboard, both in texture and in flavor. There
is not much difference in size between the sexes, but the
largest examples are always females, and a specimen eight
inches long will bring a dollar in the market.

Like many of the turtles, this one is extremely fond of
basking in the sun and is a gregarious species, so that one
often sees several individuals roosting on a log or a stone on
hot sunny afternoons. For safety reasons, they generally
select a situation well out from shore and are about as wary
as turtles can be. At the least sign of danger they all slide
into the water in a most undignified manner and become
lost amid the water weeds. This characteristic action has
given them the popular name of "sliders," although that name
is commonly applied to other species with somewhat the
same habit.

The false map turtle is less carnivorous than most of its
genus and eats a considerable amount of vegetable food. Its
jaws are not broadened and strengthened as they are in
geographica, and it is obviously not as well adapted for
crushing the shells of mollusks. However, it does feed upon
the small, thin-shelled snails and clams, and on crayfish,
worms, and various aquatic insect larvae, along with a considerable amount of the tender parts of water plants. It can

well be termed an omnivorous feeder and apparently has to have its head submerged in order to swallow.

The false map turtle is wary in the field and timid when captured. It almost never attempts to bite and will remain withdrawn in its shell for hours if it feels there is danger afoot. Young specimens are sometimes kept in goldfish bowls and are quite colorful. They will generally eat lettuce and small dead insects.

Figure 23.   Mississippi map turtle.

The Mississippi map turtle found along the coast from Texas to Mississippi, and extending up the Mississippi Valley as far as Missouri, is regarded as a subspecies of the northern turtle and is listed as *Graptemys pseudogeographica kohni* (Baur). It has higher and darker tubercles along the dorsal keel, a larger head with more powerful jaws, and there is commonly a dusky pattern on the plastron. Its habits and choice of habitat are fundamentally the same as those of the northern form, and through a large area of Missouri the two subspecies intergrade.

PAINTED TURTLE

Chrysemys picta (Schneider)

The painted turtle is one of the commonest in the country. There are several closely allied forms occupying various sections of the East, the South, the Midwest, and the Far West, so it might be said that the painted turtle is at home over practically all of the United States except the West Coast —wherever there is sufficient water. The typical subspecies, *picta picta*, occurs from the Maritime Provinces of Canada down through New England and eastern New York and Pennsylvania, all the way to northern Florida.

It is not a large turtle, most specimens averaging only five or six inches in length, with seven inches as a probable maximum. The carapace is low and broad, only slightly arched, and smooth, with no sign of a keel. The margins are smooth too. The plastron is moderately large, the connecting bridges well developed. The color ranges from olive to dull greenish black, the shields usually margined with greenish

Figure 24. Painted turtle.

yellow. The marginal shields are marked above and below with concentrically arranged black lines and bars on a red background, their lower surfaces generally quite brightly hued. The head is black with a pair of yellow spots behind the eyes, and the throat and neck are decorated with yellow stripes that change to red at the base of the neck and on the limbs and tail. The plastron may show black smudges; but in most cases it is immaculate yellow, one of the distinguishing characters for this subspecies.

This is a thoroughly aquatic turtle, seldom coming ashore, and is never likely to be found more than a few feet from some friendly body of water. It is the turtle you generally see sunning itself on a floating log, a rock projecting above the water, or perched on a tussock of grass, as you row through the lily pads on a warm summer afternoon. It is a sociable fellow, and usually several individuals are found sharing the same roost for their daily sun bath. As you approach, one will tumble into the water, followed by a couple of the others, and finally the last one will slide beneath the surface, to be lost among the muds and weeds of the bottom. The painted turtle is a lover of placid waters and is most at home in a small pond or in the coves and shallow bays of larger lakes. It has little use for streams or rivers and is seldom seen in swamps or marshes unless there are broad areas of standing water.

Their food consists of worms, aquatic insects and their larvae, fish spawn, snails, salamanders, and crustaceans. It greedily devours any dead fish or frog it chances upon. Young examples placed in an aquarium with goldfish will attack the smaller fishes; so in the wild state the painted turtle undoubtedly is a predator as well as a scavenger. Some plant material is consumed because captive specimens will eat lettuce left floating in their aquarium. Like many of our aquatic turtles, this one seems unable to swallow unless its head is underwater.

Nesting takes place in June in the northern parts of this turtle's range and in May and late April as one travels south. The site selected is generally a ridge or bank of light sandy

Figure 25.   Newly hatched painted turtles.

soil, fairly close to the water. Egg laying by this very common turtle has been observed hundreds of times.

The painted turtle hibernates early, burying itself deep in the mud of some quiet pond, and is one of the first turtles to be seen in the spring. It is a very timid species, and a freshly caught specimen will take longer to screw up enough courage to come out of its shell and start crawling than almost any other turtle of the author's experience. In photographing turtles one doesn't like to get pictures of the shell only, so after selecting a subject that is suitable it is necessary to wait until all limbs are out in the world and Mr. Turtle appears wide-awake and thoroughly alive. It certainly tries one's patience to work with this species. It is very safe to handle, for it almost never bites. Holbrook (1842) stated that its flesh is sometimes eaten, but is not "much esteemed."

The subspecies *Chrysemys picta marginata* Agassiz, called the midland painted turtle, occurs from Ontario to Michigan and Illinois, south as far as Tennessee, and east into New York and western New England. In the East it intergrades

Figure 26.   Midland painted turtle.

with the eastern form, and in the West with *belli* (see description below). The chief point of difference has to do with the shields on its carapace. The vertebral shields alternate with the costal shields, while with the typical *picta* these two sets of shields line up. The colors are the same, but the plastron generally has a darker central area.

Chrysemys picta dorsalis Agassiz, the southern painted turtle, is much the same. Its plastron, however, lacks the darker stain, and on its greenish black carapace there is a conspicuous longitudinal line down the center that is either yellowish or reddish. The marginal shields are scarcely colored above but are brightly marked with crimson and black below. This subspecies occurs in the lower Mississippi Valley, north as far as southern Illinois.

The western painted turtle, *Chrysemys picta belli* (Gray), has the most extreme range of all, being found all the way across Canada from the Great Lakes to Puget Sound in Washington. West of the Mississippi it gets down as far as Missouri and Colorado and down into New Mexico, where it

Figure 27. Western painted turtle.

crosses the border into Old Mexico. It is the largest of the group, examples more than nine inches long having been taken. The chief distinguishing character of this turtle is its plastron. The color is yellowish, with a complex pattern of black and dark gray, rather solid through the center but sending out blobs and loops along the seams.

COASTAL PLAIN TURTLE

Pseudemys floridana (LeConte)

What is generally known by herpetologists as the *"floridana* group" is divided into no less than eight subspecies, and together they occupy a range embracing practically all of our Southern states east of the Mississippi River. At the limits of their distribution, each subspecies intergrades to some extent with its neighbors, so the whole classification is most complex and far from satisfactorily worked out. What is regarded as the typical subspecies, *Pseudemys floridana floridana,* is a coastal plains form which occurs from Virginia to northern Florida and is not found very far inland.

The length of this turtle is about ten inches; but fifteen-inch specimens have been taken, so this is one of our largest pond turtles. The carapace is oval in outline and is well elevated, with its highest point about midway of the shell. The margins are smooth—not sawtoothed in the rear—and the plastron is thick and heavy, the bridges unusually robust. The color is brown, from pale to fairly dark, with a weak pattern of yellowish lines, sometimes arranged concentrically and sometimes transversely. The plastron is yellow and plain. There are usually dark blotches on the underside of the marginal shields and on the bridges. The head and limbs are brownish, more or less streaked with yellowish lines.

This turtle is popularly known as a "cooter," although the term "slider" is also used in some sections for this and almost any other species that suns itself on stumps or logs out from shore. It is at home in small ponds and swamps as well as in large lakes and rivers, and throughout its range it is a common sight to see a half-dozen or more basking on the same log.

The coastal plain turtle is mainly a vegetarian, although it will eat worms and crustaceans occasionally. When young it is much more likely to feed upon insect life, tadpoles, small mollusks, and worms. Egg laying takes place in June, the

soft-shelled eggs being more than an inch long and numbering from ten to twenty to a nest. This turtle is said to be
excellent in flavor, and it is regularly made into soup by the
fishermen throughout its range. It formerly appeared quite
commonly in the southern markets.

Pseudemys floridana concinna (LeConte) is known as
the river turtle, or the barred turtle. This subspecies ranges
well back from the coast, from Maryland south to Alabama
and west to central Tennessee. It is an inhabitant of rivers
and is seldom seen in ponds or marshes. It seems to favor a
moderately fast current and a stony bottom.

This is another large turtle, its maximum length being
about twelve inches. The color is brown, with paler markings generally arranged in a concentric pattern on each
dorsal shield. The lower side shows large dark blotches on
the marginal shields; and the plastron is yellowish, clouded
with darker shades. The fleshy parts are brown, the neck
adorned with yellowish stripes, two of them rather broad,
while the limbs bear reddish lines. The shell is long and
relatively narrow, but little arched, and weakly serrate behind.

As with most of our fresh-water turtles, this one seems to
be continually on the alert and is difficult to approach within
"grabbing range" before it dives out of sight. Although nowhere near as savage and cross-tempered as the snapping
turtle, it will bite on occasion and needs to be handled with
a bit of caution. This subspecies is considered very good
eating, and in many a southern restaurant when one orders
"diamondback terrapin" there is strong suspicion that what
he actually gets is one of these "cooters."

The hieroglyphic turtle, *Pseudemys floridana hieroglyphica* (Holbrook), is a subspecies that occurs in the Mississippi
Valley, from southern Illinois to Louisiana. To the east it
ranges to central Kentucky and Tennessee, where it intergrades with *concinna,* just discussed.

Some twelve inches in length when fully grown, this
turtle's shell is quite flat, oval in outline, the rear somewhat
flaring. The color is brown with an olive tint, and there is

Figure 28. Hieroglyphic turtle.

a network of pale yellowish lines decorating each shield, arranged in the form of bars and concentric marks. The pattern does suggest ancient writing, so the name "hieroglyphic" is very apt. The plastron is yellow, with dark shading along the seams of the plastral shields. The limbs are greenish brown with narrow yellow lines, and the head and neck are boldly marked with lines of greenish yellow, one line broadening noticeably on the neck.

Like most of its group, the hieroglyphic turtle is an omnivorous feeder. Young examples are predominantly carnivorous, living on insects, tiny mollusks, worms, and crustaceans, although known to consume some plant material. Adults are mainly herbivorous but will eat dead fish and other animal matter on occasion.

Pseudemys floridana peninsularis Carr is the form that is found through most of Florida. In this subspecies the carapace is more highly domed, with its highest point a little ahead of the middle. The rear margin is feebly notched, and the surface of the shell is quite smooth. The color is dull greenish black, the pattern of paler lines and reticula-

Figure 29. Peninsular turtle.

tions being very faint and sometimes not discernible at all.
There are a few dark blotches on the lower side of the marginal shields, with those toward the rear generally being
unmarked. The plastron is uniformly greenish white. The
head, neck, and the limbs are nearly black, with greenish
yellow lines.

This subspecies occurs in ponds, swamps, ditches, lakes,
and sluggish rivers—anywhere there is relatively quiet water
and an abundance of aquatic vegetation. It is herbivorous
in habits, at least in the adult stage, and lives chiefly upon
the abundant and lush plant life of its semitropical environment. Specimens are often seen feeding upon scraps of
melon and other fruit that has been cast into the water.

On the Gulf Coast of Florida, above St. Petersburg and
extending well along the panhandle, we find still another
subspecies of the *floridana* complex, this one listed as
Pseudemys floridana suwanniensis Carr. It is popularly
known as the Suwannee turtle, or often as the "Suwannee
Chicken."

Figure 30. Suwannee turtle.

This is probably the largest of any of the subspecies, examples more than sixteen inches long being recorded. The shell is elongate and well arched, rounded before and weakly serrate behind, and flaring a little at the posterior margins. The plastron is long and relatively narrow, the connecting bridges wide and sturdy. The color is dark greenish black, and any markings on the carapace are faint indeed. There are dark smudgy rings on the lower sides of the marginals and on the bridges, with the plastron greenish white, more or less blotched with darker tones along the seams of the shields. The limbs are greenish black with narrow yellowish lines, and the head and neck are the same color but are usually more plainly marked with greenish yellow lines.

One strange thing about this subspecies is its tolerance for widely varied conditions of salinity in its home waters. It is abundant in crystal-clear springs and perhaps even more abundant in shallow marine waters. In some places it has been seen by the hundreds feeding upon turtle grass in shallow lagoons and coves at the mouths of rivers, such feeding grounds commonly being known as "turtle meadows." It is not uncommon to find a specimen whose shell is encrusted with barnacles.

It is one of the most socially minded of all turtles, and many travelers have described areas of cypress ponds with literally thousands of the reptiles sunning themselves, several dozen to a log or stump, often pyramided two or three deep. Other writers have reported hundreds of heads of this turtle thrust above the surface in shallow salt water covering grassy flats. As the popular name of "Suwannee Chicken" would imply, this is one of the best of all southern turtles for eating purposes; and it is reported to make the best stew of any Florida pond turtle.

Along the Gulf Coast from northwestern Florida through Alabama and Louisiana, the subspecies *Pseudemys floridana mobiliensis* Carr is found. This is another large form, attaining a length of fourteen or fifteen inches, with the average specimen just about one foot long. In shape and general appearance it is much like the last one, *suwanniensis*, but its predominant color is brown instead of black, and the narrow lines or stripes on the fleshy parts are tinted with orange instead of being pale greenish yellow. There is generally a pattern of dark spots or blotches on the plastron.

This subspecies lives near the coastal areas and, like *suwanniensis*, appears to be as perfectly at home in brackish estuaries as it does in clear waters further inland and is frequently seen swimming about or feeding in shallow marine waters. It is well regarded as a food item throughout its range.

Pseudemys floridana hoyi (Agassiz) is the form found west of the Mississippi River, from southern Kansas and Missouri south through Arkansas and Oklahoma to well down into Texas. This turtle does not get quite as big as some of its Eastern relatives, and one that is ten inches long represents a really large specimen.

The shell of this subspecies is somewhat rectangular in outline and not very highly elevated. The plastron is large, the bridges wide and sturdy. The color is dark slate-gray, with a series of yellowish bars and lines decorating the upper surface, while the plastron is pale yellowish to nearly white. The limbs and head bear numerous thin yellowish lines.

The popular name of this turtle should probably be Hoy's turtle, but in our Middle Western states it is pretty generally called the saw-toothed slider. It may be found in ponds and lakes and in the quieter portions of streams and rivers, its chief concern being a soft muddy bottom and an abundance of vegetation. It climbs out on objects for sun bathing and also likes to bask just at the surface, perhaps partially supported by submerged water weeds, with just its head above the water.

In this group of turtles, as well as with others, the males may be distinguished by the length of the claws on their front feet. They are frequently two or three times longer in the case of male turtles. This subspecies, *hoyi*, sometimes carries this difference to extremes, and occasionally one finds an example with two or more claws projecting like toothpicks for as much as a couple of inches. Folks used to believe that these elongated nails were used by the turtle to fish worms out of their burrows, but if this were true the lady turtles would certainly be at a disadvantage in food gathering. It is now known that they simply have some function during the courtship season.

The remaining subspecies of the *floridana* group is the Texas sawback, *Pseudemys floridana texana* Baur, which is found in southern and western Texas as well as in northern Mexico. Its length is from eight to ten inches; and its shell is oval, moderately arched, and highest at its center. The upper beak is notched in front. The color is olive brown with a network of orange or whitish lines and reticulations, not very evident in mature specimens but quite striking in juveniles. The marginal shields bear rings and half-circles of the same shade on the upper surface, while underneath they show dark rings, one within another. The plastron is pale yellow. The head and neck are decorated with a complex pattern of broken lines, bars, and spots.

The Texas sawback is found in rivers, ponds, ditches, and

often in the water tanks on ranches. Its habits are essentially the same as those of its neighboring subspecies *hoyi*, with which it freely intergrades.

RED-BELLIED TURTLE

Pseudemys rubriventris (LeConte)

This colorful turtle occupies a somewhat restricted range in the Northeast, being found from southern New York along the coastal plain to south-central Virginia. A subspecies is known from Massachusetts.

This is one of our largest "sliders" and may be the largest of that group. Ten- and eleven-inch specimens are not too uncommon, and at least one individual of fifteen inches has been recorded. The shell is elongate-oval and rather flat, its highest point just back of the middle. The rear margin is only feebly serrate, the plastron is ample, and the connecting bridges wide and sturdy. The carapace is unkeeled and is generally wrinkled at the sides. The beak is notched, with a prominent hook on both sides. The tail is quite short, and the feet are strongly webbed.

The color is olive brown, more or less reticulated with red in young specimens and with yellowish gray in mature shells. There is a red bar present in each marginal shield, and sometimes the costal shields show blotches or spots of red. The plastron is orange-red, unmarked in adults but spotted with black in youngsters. The head and limbs are greenish black, with a complex pattern of narrow red and black lines. As with many of our turtles, the most vividly marked examples are partly grown individuals.

This is a turtle of both streams and ponds. It may be found in swift-flowing rivers where the bottom is stony or gravelly, and it is just as likely to be seen in some small pond with a muddy bottom. It occurs in the brackish mouths of streams flowing into the sea and has been taken in salt marshes. In any case, it is a very wary animal which is difficult to approach and not at all easy to capture. Like the other "sliders" it is an inveterate sun bather, but it invariably chooses a site well out from shore where there is deep water handy in which it can take refuge. It leaves its perch and heads for safety quicker than almost any other species.

The red-bellied turtle is another omnivorous feeder. Captive specimens accept fruit, vegetables, fish, and meat with equal relish. In the wild state they probably consume various aquatic plants, along with the common turtle diet of worms, insects, crustaceans, mollusks, and carrion. It is usually a gentle creature, seldom attempting to bite; however, a turtle this big should be handled with due caution, as one never can predict what a particular individual may do.

The eggs are deposited in June in sand, clay, or loam—a sandy loam being most frequently selected. A cornfield adjoining the water offers an ideal situation for their nesting. From eight to fifteen eggs are laid in a vase-shaped excavation, after which the female scrapes earth into the neck of the hole and does such a good job of smoothing it over that the nest is hard to find.

At the turn of the century, when diamondback terrapins were in such popular demand, this species was often substituted for them when diamondbacks were scarce. It is still used for food to a limited extent in localities where it is moderately plentiful and is said to have an excellent flavor, but in most places it is not an abundant species.

A subspecies of the red-bellied turtle, *Pseudemys rubriventris bangsi* Babcock, lives as an isolated group in a few ponds in Plymouth County, Massachusetts. In his *New England Turtles* (1919) Babcock lists them from several ponds on Cape Cod and records that they were fairly abundant at some spots, but they are probably rare in New England today.

FLORIDA RED-BELLIED TURTLE

Pseudemys nelsoni Carr

This is another large turtle, resembling quite closely the one just described, but its range is confined to peninsular Florida. Its length may be as much as thirteen inches, and

Figure 31.   Florida red-bellied turtle.

it differs from the red-bellied turtle of the north by having
a much higher carapace and a much more rugged bridge between the shell parts. The general color is dark brown or
nearly black, more or less marked with reddish scrawls and
wedge-shaped smudges. The plastron is red or orange-red
in most cases but may be yellowish, and it is without spots or
blotches in the adult stage.

This turtle occurs in clear streams, in muddy ponds and
ditches, and in the mangrove swamps along the coast. It is
generally found in the company of turtles of other species,
commonly sharing the same logs or stumps with them on
sunny afternoons. It is largely vegetarian in habits, but it
will eat dead fish and no doubt consumes a few crustaceans
and worms when they are available. Captive specimens
show a decided preference for water plants such as the water
hyacinth and *Sagittaria*.

This species is a comparative newcomer to the list of
American turtles, the first specimen having been described
and named by Dr. Archie Carr in 1938. Before that date the
red-bellied turtle of Florida was regarded as the same as the

northern form, and the range of that form was given as "New England to Florida," but Dr. Carr demonstrated that the Florida turtle is entitled to full specific rank.

YELLOW-BELLIED TURTLE

Pseudemys scripta (Schoepff)

This is another of the "sliders"; and the *scripta* group, with its subspecies, embraces a territory covering most of our Southern and Central states. The typical form, which should be listed as *Pseudemys scripta scripta,* ranges from southeastern Virginia down through the Carolinas and Georgia to nearly central Florida and west through the Florida panhandle to southern Alabama.

Its length averages about nine inches, although specimens nearly eleven inches in length have been reported. The shell is broadly oval in outline and slightly arched. There is a weak keel on the back, but this is not often evident in older, worn shells. The rear margins are rather strongly

Figure 32. Yellow-bellied turtle.

toothed. The costal shields are decorated with prominent longitudinal wrinkles, especially near the margins. The plastron is large, the bridges wide and heavy.

The color is dark greenish black above, with a weak pattern of paler bars or lines on some of the shields. The plastron is yellow and immaculate, but there is a large black spot or smudge on the lower side of each of the marginal shields. The head and limbs are greenish olive, the head and neck bearing yellow stripes. Two of these stripes fuse just back of the eye to form a conspicuous broad yellow patch.

The yellow-bellied turtle prefers small ponds and muddy pools, although it may be found in relatively quiet streams and in the shallow coves of lakes. It does not appear to be as gregarious as most of the sliders, and one rarely encounters several individuals taking a sun bath on the same derelict log. More frequently single specimens are seen at rather widely separated places. It appears to tolerate polluted conditions almost as well as a musk turtle and thrives in some localities where increasing pollution has forced the more particular species, such as *Pseudemys floridana*, to vacate.

In food habits this turtle is somewhat omnivorous, probably with a leaning toward being carnivorous. It is known to eat crayfish, shrimps, worms, and larvae of aquatic insects; is occasionally taken on a baited hook; and has been observed feeding upon submerged water plants. This species lays its eggs in May or June, the number about a dozen. They are elliptical and hard shelled and are deposited in a flask-shaped hole that is dug by the female, usually not far from the water's edge. They hatch in the late summer.

Pseudemys scripta elegans (Wied) is known as the red-eared turtle, or the elegant turtle. This subspecies is at home in the Mississippi Valley, ranging north into Illinois and Iowa, east as far as central Ohio and Tennessee, and west through Colorado and Texas.

This is one of the easiest of our fresh-water turtles to identify, owing to the conspicuous red patch behind its eye, a mark that is present from infancy. The carapace is low

Figure 33. Red-eared turtle. *Inset:* The long nails of the male.

and rather flat, unkeeled or very feebly keeled, and serrate behind. The plastron is large and sturdy, the bridge wide and strong. As with many of our turtles, the male is smaller than the female and may be distinguished by its longer and more curving claws on the forefeet.

The color of the carapace is olive green, with yellowish and black lines running transversely across the shell. The marginal shields usually bear rings or half-circles of yellow. The plastron may be uniform yellowish, or it may vary from light to heavily spotted or marbled with black. The undersides of the marginals show black rings or smudges, and the bridge is also smeared with blackish marks. The head, the neck, and the limbs are striped with greenish yellow, and just back of the eye is the aforementioned red patch that identifies this subspecies.

Young, newly hatched examples of this turtle are gaily marked little fellows, their shells showing a beautiful pattern of greenish ocellated markings above and symmetrically arranged black circles below, with the conspicuous red neck-patch much in evidence. They are the favorite species found in pet shops and five-and-dime stores, and many thousands are sold each year.

This turtle likes to live in larger ponds and lakes and in quieter parts of rivers, such as the oxbows so prevalent along portions of the Mississippi. At the same time it may be found in smaller prairie ponds and sloughs, its chief concern being a low marshy shoreline with an abundance of weedy vegetation. It spends most of its time in the water, apparently seldom venturing on land except at egg-laying time. If they are at all common in a locality, every log or stone jutting out from shore will be covered with them on sunny days, sometimes piled two or three deep. They are wary animals, and the first suggestion of danger sends the whole bunch "sliding" into the water and safety.

When young this subspecies is largely carnivorous, feeding upon all sorts of aquatic insects, worms, and snails; but in the adult stage it consumes a great deal of vegetable matter. It is a mild-mannered turtle as a rule, although some individuals will make a half-hearted attempt to bite when handled. From four or five to as many as twenty oval, leathery-shelled eggs are deposited in the spring, generally along some ridge of loose soil adjoining the water.

CHICKEN TURTLE

Deirochelys reticularia (Latreille)

The chicken turtle is found from eastern North Carolina south throughout Florida, west along the coastal plain as far as Texas, and north to Oklahoma and Arkansas. It gets its popular name from the fact that its flesh is considered excellent in flavor. In fact, it is the best of our fresh-water turtles and has always been a favorite species for the table.

The maximum size for this turtle is said to be about ten inches, but the average specimen is between six and eight. The carapace is oval and well elevated, not notched behind; and the large plastron has a distinct notch between the two anal shields. The upper surface bears a distinctive reticulate

Figure 34. Chicken turtle.

pattern of narrow, wrinkle-like furrows that are usually pale in color on an olive-brown background. The plastron is yellow, with one or two black blotches on the bridges; and there may be a dark smudge on the lower side of the marginal shields. The head and neck are olive brown, with varying longitudinal greenish streaks, while the limbs are clouded with yellow or pale green. There is a characteristic pattern of vertical stripes on the rump. Because the neck of this turtle is unusually long, one of the popular names for it is "long-necked turtle."

The chicken turtle inhabits small ponds, roadside ditches, sluggish streams, and stagnant pools and is a sociable creature, several individuals often being seen basking on the same fallen log at the water's edge. Excessively timid, they all plunge into the water at the slightest alarm; and the splash of the first one appears to warn all others within hearing, so that often when surprising one group the intruder hears a succession of splashes leading off in the distance, telling of other turtles, still out of sight, that are heading for safety. It is a common sight to see two or three of these long-necked turtles swimming slowly along in shallow water, with just their heads above the surface, and the resemblance to a group of water snakes is striking.

Although primarily an aquatic reptile, this species shows a decided liking for wandering about on land, and not necessarily in swampy or marshy situations either. It is sometimes encountered some distance from any water and is one of the commonest turtles to be found killed by motorists on Florida highways.

The chicken turtle is probably an omnivorous feeder. Captive specimens are not at all "choosy" about their food, taking strips of fish, beef, or certain vegetables with equal relish. It is known to eat crayfish and has been observed catching and devouring a tadpole. No doubt its natural diet includes worms, mollusks, and carrion, as well as a fair amount of plant life. Egg laying may take place at any time in the summer or fall, at least in Florida. A captive specimen of the author's (in Connecticut) laid two eggs on July 15 and 16. The female conceals her eggs in a hole that she digs, often in a plowed field near some swampy area, the clutch numbering from seven to fifteen.

While this turtle demonstrates that it is unusually timid in a wild state, it is not as mild mannered as most of our pond turtles and is more likely to nip your finger if you pick it up carelessly. Most examples become tame very quickly, however, and make very satisfactory pets. The peculiarly furrowed appearance of the carapace sets the chicken turtle apart from other pond turtles and makes it easy to identify.

GOPHER TORTOISE

Gopherus polyphemus (Daudin)

The gopher tortoise is a completely terrestrial animal, occurring from southwestern South Carolina to near the southern tip of Florida. Westward it ranges through southern Georgia, Alabama, and Mississippi to Louisiana, just getting into the states of Texas and Arkansas.

This is a large species, attaining a length of almost fourteen inches and a weight of from ten to twelve pounds. It has been said to reach a length of eighteen inches, but there is no authentic record of a specimen that big. The shell is moderately elongate, highly arched—almost dome-shaped—but is flattened a little at the top. It is bluntly rounded at both front and rear. In old specimens the surface is quite smooth; but with young individuals there are many sharp, concentric grooves on each shield. The plastron is thick and heavy, with very wide bridges, serving well to protect the reptile's underside. The head and limbs are solid and strong, the feet not webbed. The general carapace color is dull yellowish brown, the plastron dull yellowish. The fleshy parts are grayish brown.

The gopher tortoise derives its name from the fact that it digs burrows in which to live, after the fashion of the rodents of the same name. In sandy areas of our southland these "gopher holes" are common, and several quite unrelated animals have come to depend on them for more or less permanent homes. Probably the best known are the gopher frog and the gopher snake, the latter more properly referred to as the indigo snake. Both of these cold-blooded creatures appear to prefer a cavelike retreat for escaping the heat of

Figure 35. Gopher tortoise.

summer days and are commonly found well back from the
entrance of some gopher burrow. Many other animals take
advantage of these ready-made homes during bad weather;

and the list of creatures that have been found in them includes lizards, salamanders, opossums, rabbits, raccoons, foxes, and snakes of many kinds, including rattlers. Hosts of various insects are also occasional "guests."

As mentioned before, the gopher tortoises prefer dry and sandy places in which to live; and the burrow corresponds pretty much to the size of the tortoise that constructs it. Young specimens excavate burrows slightly larger than the dimensions of their shells and perhaps three or four feet deep, while large individuals may produce a burrow a foot or more wide and as much as thirty feet in length. The burrow runs obliquely in the ground for several feet, then levels off, and is enlarged into a chamber at its end. The tortoises are most active in the early morning and again in the late afternoon, spending the hot midday hours in these cool underground retreats.

The gopher tortoise is a vegetarian in the main, although it is known to eat insects occasionally. Its principal food is made up of grasses and the leaves of low shrubs, with some fruits. In captivity they will eat lettuce and celery and are reported to be very fond of watermelon and cantaloupe rinds.

Egg laying takes place any time from April to July. A shallow excavation is scooped in the sandy soil some five or six inches deep, sometimes right at the entrance of a burrow but more frequently some distance away. Here are deposited five or six almost spherical eggs about an inch and a half in diameter. They are hard shelled and white in color. The newly hatched tortoises are extremely secretive and are very seldom observed. Many nests are dug up and destroyed by rodents and other predators, and in some sections of the south the eggs are commonly eaten by man.

The gopher tortoise is an inoffensive creature, gentle in habits, and never appears to entertain any thoughts about biting. It thrives in captivity, and examples will live for years in almost any sort of enclosure that they cannot dig under; although, strangely enough, in a roomy enclosure this "digginest" of turtles rarely makes any attempt to exca-

vate a burrow. Holbrook (1842) stated that captive specimens showed an almost panicky dislike for rain and would
scurry for cover at the first signs of an approaching shower.
However, gopher tortoises are among the commonest of
animals at roadside "animal farms" in Florida; and the author has many times observed them placidly going about
their business during moderately heavy rains, with dry cover
within easy reach.

In earlier days the flesh of this tortoise was regularly consumed in many parts of the South, and it was not unusual to
see examples displayed for sale in country stores. No doubt
an occasional specimen finds its way into the family pot today, but it is not eaten to any extent.

These reptiles are allied to the giant land tortoises of the
Galapagos Islands, which weigh as much as three hundred
pounds and have no trouble in carrying a full-grown man on
their back. These enormous creatures hold the record for
longevity, probably exceeding 150 years; and it is very likely
that our gopher tortoises, barring accidents, have a longer
life expectancy than any of the birds or mammals that share
their range.

TEXAS GOPHER TORTOISE

Gopherus berlandieri (Agassiz)

This species is much like the common gopher tortoise of
our southern coastal regions. The shell is less elongate—in
other words, more rounded—and the head and limbs are proportionally smaller than with *polyphemus*. Also, this tortoise does not grow to so large a size, about eight inches
being its maximum length. It is found in southeastern Texas
and extends well down into Mexico.

Like its Eastern relative, this fellow prefers well-drained,
sandy soils and digs lengthy burrows for resting purposes
wherever the terrain will permit it. In hard-packed clay
and in stony country they seem to get along nicely with

merely a shallow depression, or they find a snug retreat under some stump or tangle of debris.

The Texas gopher tortoise feeds chiefly on fruits of the cactus during the summer months. At other seasons it eats blossoms, tender young leaves, various grasses, and some insects. Its general habits are substantially the same as those of the common gopher tortoise.

DESERT TORTOISE

Gopherus agassizi (Cooper)

The desert tortoise is at home in southern California and southwestern Arizona, ranging south into Mexico and north as far as southern Nevada and Utah. As its popular name indicates, it is a creature of desert and semidesert country, at home in dry, sandy, or gravelly territory, the land of cactus and mesquite.

The carapace is dome shaped and elongate, the sides nearly parallel, and it is somewhat serrate behind. The plastron adequately protects the reptile's lower side and is provided with a pair of shields, both fore and aft, that project beyond the rest of the shell in a marked manner. The ones in front are particularly apparent, reminding one of the prow of a boat, and are called gular projections. They are most pronounced on old and mature individuals. The limbs are sturdy and heavily scaled, the hind pair being especially robust and flat on the bottom like a miniature elephant's foot.

When the desert tortoise withdraws into its shell the hard soles of its hind feet block the area between the carapace and the plastron, affording fine protection to the rear of the reptile. The forelegs have very tough scales on their front surface, so that when they are drawn into the shell they seal off that end of the tortoise as well. As the head is drawn back into the shell the forelegs come together in front, and the tortoise is provided with an almost invincible armor.

Figure 36. Desert tortoise.

The maximum length of this species is thirteen and one-half inches. Its chief points of difference from the other gopher tortoises are its noticeably smaller head and its much larger hind feet.

Like most tortoises, this one is a noted burrower. More-over, this species digs two different types of burrow. In gravel banks and on dry sandy hillsides, it may construct a burrow as much as thirty feet long, with a roomy chamber at the end. This is used for hibernation during the winter months, and several individuals commonly share a single burrow. The other type is an individual affair, generally no more than five feet deep and rather sharply inclined. Here the tortoise retires during the hot summer days to escape the heat, doing most of its foraging early in the morning and late in the afternoon, although it is ordinarily not nocturnal. All of the tortoise's digging is done with the front feet.

At mating time the males often stage determined fights. They meet head-on and each endeavors to overturn its rival by getting the gular projection of its plastron under his rival's shell and then lifting. Back and forth the adversaries struggle, each straining to the utmost until one becomes dis-couraged and backs away from the contest, or until one of the contestants is upset. The victor then goes off in search of the female which is certain to be close at hand, while the vanquished sets about the task of getting itself right-side up again. If the soil should be loose so that the tortoise cannot get leverage to use its head for the push-over, and the desert sun is bright, the animal may die within a short time.

The desert tortoise is a mild-mannered and harmless creature; and it is too bad that so many specimens each year are picked up by tourists and brought back to Eastern states, where they rarely live more than a few months. In its desert environment it will live for years in captivity, feeding upon almost any kind of vegetables and fruits. The old-time cow-boys would never kill one of these tortoises unnecessarily, as it was one animal that a man could capture in the event he was lost on the desert without a gun; and it might very well save his life from starvation or thirst. In the north woods the same unwritten law is observed by woodsmen in regard to the porcupine.

SOUTHERN SOFT-SHELLED TURTLE

Trionyx ferox (Schneider)

The soft-shelled turtles form an interesting group, quite different from one's usual concept of what a turtle should look like. The shell is not really "soft"; in fact, it is fairly hard over the back, but its rim is more or less flexible. The carapace is not divided into shields but is covered by a sort of leathery skin. We have two species in this country. One is the *ferox* group (with six subspecies), characterized by small bumps or tubercles along the front edge of the carapace and generally referred to as the spiny soft-shelled turtles; and the other is the *muticus* group, which is without these decorations. Both species are about as completely aquatic as a fresh-water turtle can be.

The southern soft-shell, *Trionyx ferox ferox* (Schneider), ranges through all of Florida except the western part of the panhandle and extends north into southern Georgia. This is our largest variety of soft-shelled turtles, individuals up to eighteen inches long being known. Around the front of the carapace is a sort of fringe of small conical tubercles, a characteristic mark of the *ferox* group. The whole animal is rather flat, the back hardly arched at all; and the shell is somewhat circular in outline, only a little longer than it is wide and is often marked with longitudinal wrinkles, particularly toward the edges. The limbs are sturdy and fully webbed at the end but are not much unlike those of the hard-shelled turtles. The neck is very long; and the head is distinctly pointed, ending in a flexible, proboscis-like snout. A really big specimen may weigh up to thirty pounds.

In color this species is dull brown, sometimes marbled with black. The plastron, which seems to protect the front part of the animal more than it does the rear, is immaculate white. The limbs are olive brown above and pale gray to whitish below; and the head and neck are brown, with a yellowish band on each side. These bands extend up through the eyes and unite on top of the head, a short distance in

Figure 37. *Above:* Southern soft-shelled turtle. *Below:* Head of a soft-shelled turtle.

front of the eyes. The young are colorful little fellows, yellowish gray (above), strongly marked with a pattern of dusky spots, usually dispersed in rings. Sometimes these circles are so large that only small patches of the yellow ground color can be seen.

This turtle is a superb swimmer and is seldom seen out of water. It occasionally basks in the sun on some slime-covered log, and in the spring it has to crawl a few feet ashore to lay its eggs, but the adult turtle is a rather awkward animal on dry land. On the other hand, young and partly grown examples are surprisingly agile on land and can actually run along the ground at a fairly rapid rate. In life the soft-shelled turtle spends a large part of its time buried in the oozy mud, with just its head protruding. They like to lie in only a few inches of water, periodically stretching their unusually long necks to the surface for a gulp of air.

This turtle shows considerable tolerance for environmental conditions. It is common in lakes and rivers, muddy canals and ponds, at the mouths of streams where the waters are brackish, and in the clearest of springs. Those people who have had the good fortune to visit Silver Springs in Florida and taken the famous glass-bottom boat ride there have most certainly seen them swimming gracefully about in the crystal-clear waters.

Soft-shelled turtles are largely carnivorous, feeding upon fish, frogs, young water birds, worms, mollusks, and insects and crustaceans. In many places they are considered pests by fishermen, as they often gulp worms and find themselves fast on the end of some angler's line. They are said to have a temper as savage as that of a snapping turtle, and their long flexible necks enable them to strike with the speed of a snake. The jaws are by no means "soft" and are capable of inflicting a painful wound.

Nesting takes place any time from March to June. The female scoops out a cavity in the sand a few feet above the shore line and completely buries herself with only her snout visible. Here she stays until the eggs are all laid, a task that may require several days. The eggs number from fifteen to twenty, are white in color, have thin brittle shells, and are perfectly spherical. Their diameter is about one inch. Many, probably the majority, nests are destroyed by roving skunks, raccoons, and opossums.

This turtle thrives well in captivity, if provided with a suitable tank to live in, but it is a voracious feeder and requires a plentiful supply of dead fish and frogs if it is to be maintained in good health. The flesh is of excellent flavor, this being one of our most edible turtles.

The Carolina soft-shelled turtle, *Trionyx ferox agassizi* (Baur), ranges from southern Georgia to about central North Carolina, keeping pretty close to the coastal plains areas. When partly grown the carapace is more heavily spotted than in the one just discussed, but with old specimens it takes an expert to tell them apart, and frequently the experts are uncertain unless they know exactly where the individual came from. It does not grow to as large a size as the Florida soft-shell, about fourteen inches being its greatest length. In habits they are essentially the same, with the Carolina subspecies showing a strong preference for rivers.

The Gulf Coast soft-shelled turtle, *Trionyx ferox aspera* (Agassiz), occupies a range that embraces most of Alabama and Mississippi, the western edge of northern Florida, and the eastern half of Louisiana. It is only slightly different from the Florida subspecies and intergrades freely with it in northwest Florida as well as with *agassizi* in western Georgia. The tubercles at the front of the shell are perhaps longer, and there are slight differences in the neck stripes.

Trionyx ferox emoryi (Agassiz), the Texas soft-shelled turtle, is found all across the southern section of the country, from Louisiana to eastern California, occupying most of Texas and ranging well down into Mexico. It may be distinguished from the others by its nostrils, which are concentric rather than rounded. This subspecies attains a length of some fifteen inches and is found chiefly in rivers, although it occurs to some extent in ponds and reservoirs.

The eastern spiny soft-shelled turtle, *Trionyx ferox spinifera* (LeSueur), is the common form and is perhaps the best known of the whole group. It occurs from Minnesota to Vermont in the northern limits of its range and south as far as Tennessee. In the Mississippi Valley it occurs all the way down to the Gulf of Mexico. In earlier days it was regarded as a distinct species and was listed as *Trionyx spinifera*, with the *ferox* left out.

This is a smaller turtle than its southern relatives, attaining a maximum length of about fourteen inches. The carapace is dull olive brown, with a yellowish black-lined border. Numerous black rings and blotches adorn the upper surface, while the underside is milky-white. The head is olive brown, and the narrow yellow neck-stripes extend through the eyes and connect on the snout, instead of just in front of the eyes, as with the Florida soft-shell. As with many of our turtles, young and partly grown examples show distinct spotting, while old individuals are likely to be dull colored, the spots changed to irregular cloudings.

This turtle is at home in rivers and lakes and ponds, anywhere it can find soft bottom conditions, for it too likes to lie in the mud with only its snout exposed. It has been theorized that this persistent habit is one reason why it has developed a softer shell, for it does not have as much need for a hard protective covering. The long rubbery neck and the tube-like snout with its wide nasal openings are probably adaptations to this mode of life.

On warm sunny days, however, this turtle likes to crawl out on some flat stone or log to bask in the sun. A spot well away from shore is selected for obvious reasons, and very often several individuals will share the same stone. They are alert and wary, and it is seldom possible to approach nearer than fifty yards before they all slip silently into the water. Like all the soft-shelled turtles, this one is almost as expert in the water as a sea turtle. Old and mature specimens are not at all comfortable on land, but partly grown examples are surprisingly quick in their movements ashore. Young individuals, especially, run with commendable rapidity, high on their legs, belying the proverbial slowness of the tortoise.

The food of this subspecies is made up of crustaceans and the larvae of dragonflies and other aquatic insects, along with fish, frogs, small mollusks, and worms. Carrion is readily accepted and probably some plant material, although they are not regarded as vegetarians. It, too, often swallows a worm and finds itself hooked by some excited fisherman who probably thinks he has caught the largest fish in the river until it is reeled in.

This subspecies has pretty much the same habits of nesting, food gathering, etc., as its southern relatives and also does well in captivity if properly fed and cared for. It, too, has a diabolical disposition, strikes savagely when cornered, and needs to be handled with respect.

The western soft-shelled turtle, *Trionyx ferox hartwegi* Conant and Goin, ranges west of the Mississippi River, from Montana down through Wyoming and the Dakotas to Louisiana. All along the Mississippi it intergrades with the eastern subspecies just discussed. The chief point of difference between the two appears to be the markings on their backs. In this western subspecies the carapace is dotted with round marks that are nearly all the same size, while with *spinifera* those near the center of the shell are distinctly larger. This is mainly a river turtle, at home in the Mississippi and Missouri rivers and their many tributaries. Its habits, and indeed its appearance, are about the same as those of its eastern cousin. Throughout the territory covered by the two subspecies, they are the best by far for eating purposes, only slightly inferior to the celebrated diamondback of the Atlantic states and very definitely superior to any of the cooters or sliders.

SMOOTH SOFT-SHELLED TURTLE

Trionyx muticus LeSueur

This is probably our smallest soft-shelled turtle, averaging only seven or eight inches in length, although it has been known to attain a length of nearly fourteen inches. It is perhaps a bit more circular in outline (as an adult) than those of the *ferox* group, and the front edge of the carapace is without any bumps or tubercles. Another point of difference is in the circular nasal openings at the end of the snout, which in the *muticus* are not separated by a ridge-like septum. Otherwise the reptile is low and flat like the others and obviously meant for living in the water. Natives in many parts of its range call it the "pancake turtle," although that vernacular name is used as well for any of soft-shelled group.

The upper surface is olive brown, with irregular blotches of a darker shade, and usually with a paler band around the border. The underside is grayish white, with the fleshy parts gray, more or less mottled with brown. There is a black-edged line of yellow along the neck, passing through the eye.

The smooth soft-shelled turtle is at home in the central part of the country, chiefly along the Mississippi and Ohio rivers and the many creeks and streams that flow into them. To the east it gets into Ohio and ranges to the north as far as southern Minnesota and Michigan. Westward it is found from central Texas up to South Dakota, while to the south it occurs as far as central Louisiana. In many parts of its range it shares the same territory with various members of the *ferox* group but never intergrades with them and can easily be distinguished by the smoothness of its front end. It is less common than the spiny soft-shells and is not nearly so frequently collected.

This is primarily a turtle of rivers. It shows a marked preference for moderately fast, clear streams with sandy or gravelly bottoms, although it occurs to some extent in slow-moving, muddy-bottomed rivers. It is not very often encountered in lakes or ponds and almost never in the standing waters of sloughs, ditches, or canals. Like the other soft-shells, it delights in concealing itself in the sand in a few inches of water, just deep enough so it can reach the surface for an occasional breath of air by extending its long neck. It is not known to crawl out on stones or logs for sun bathing, but it may now and then rest on some grassy or sandy bank right at the edge of the water.

We might say, in fact, that this is the most thoroughly aquatic of all the soft-shelled turtles and, if we exclude the sea turtles, it is no doubt the most "water loving" of any American turtle. It goes without saying that it is an excellent swimmer, graceful, speedy, and extremely agile. It has been known to chase down and capture a brook trout in a large tank, although it probably would not be that successful under natural conditions. At the same time it is not too ungainly on land and is capable of vigorous and brisk movements ashore—even though it seldom leaves the water by its own choice.

Crayfish and aquatic insect larvae make up the bulk of its diet, supplemented by worms, thin-shelled mollusks, frogs, and fish. It is commonly accused of being very destructive to fish life in general; and most fishermen regard the soft-shell as a mortal enemy, or at least as a strong and successful competitor. More than likely, however, any inroads these turtles make on the fish population of a river are comparatively minor; and a fair proportion of the fish found in the stomach of any soft-shelled turtle represents specimens that were already dead when the reptile found them, for the soft-shell is a noted scavenger as well as a predator. A small amount of vegetable matter is also consumed.

The eggs are laid in June or early July, and may number as many as thirty, the average nest containing from fifteen to twenty. The eggs are spherical, white, and measure somewhat less than one inch in diameter. The site selected for nesting is never more than a few feet from water and is apt to be fairly free of vegetation, so that a good view may be had in all directions. Perhaps the favorite situation is on some sand bar, with water on both sides. Like the other soft-shelled turtles, the female *muticus* buries herself completely with just her head above the sand, and stays in place until the job is completed.

The sharp beak is capable of inflicting a painful wound, and it is backed up by a thoroughly nasty disposition, so this species needs to be handled with care. The safest way to carry a specimen is by its tail. The smooth soft-shelled turtle is just as good to eat as the spiny varieties, and it does quite well in captivity. Baby examples, with their boldly spotted shells and active ways, make particularly interesting pets.

THE MARINE TURTLES

Many millions of years ago the first air-breathing animals came into being, amphibians that could live out of water a good share of the time, but which still had to return to the water to lay their eggs, for the young were invariably gill-breathers. In due time, some ancestral amphibian group gave rise to the first primitive reptiles; and eventually the world was populated by creatures that were completely independent of the sea. They could carry on all of life's activities —food-gathering, courtship, egg laying—without ever going near the water.

Strangely enough, however, some of these animals returned to the sea and developed into efficient marine animals, their bodies becoming adapted for a watery existence. It is a law of evolution that a structure once lost can never be regained; so these animals, having returned to a life in the sea, can never redevelop gills. They must forever come to the surface periodically for oxygen. We see classic examples of marine creatures whose forebears lived on land in the whales, dolphins, and porpoises; but other groups are less completely aquatic. In addition to being dependent on oxygen from the air they must return to the land in order to lay their eggs or to have their young. Examples of this kind of sea creature would be the sea snakes, seals and walruses, and the marine turtles.

These huge sea turtles have gone a long way in their chosen medium, finding both food and safety at sea; and only the need for egg laying brings them to land at all. This annual shoreward migration is fraught with dire peril which nothing but the most urgent summons would cause them to face. There is reason to believe, moreover, that in some species the males never come ashore at all.

All of the tropical and semitropical seas are inhabited by huge turtles, which are divided into two major groups. The largest of them all, the leatherback turtle, appears to be the only survivor of an almost extinct race; while all the others trace their ancestry back to types that were not unlike our modern fresh-water turtles.

The limbs are all converted into large, paddle-like organs, the toes generally lost or concealed by a common skin. The forelimbs are always considerably larger than the hind pair. The head is massive and heavy, flattened above, with jaws that are horny, very sharp, and beaklike. The bony case of these animals is too small for the reception of the head and limbs; and these parts are, consequently, always more or less protruding. Most of the sea turtles feed upon seaweeds, but a few devour mollusks and other marine animals. The flesh of the vegetarians affords a wholesome and delicious food; and they are in consequence much sought after, while that of the carnivorous species is disagreeable and even unwholesome. They are only collected for the sake of the abundant supply of oil which they yield.

Some of the prehistoric turtles grew to a tremendous size, dwarfing any sea turtle of modern times. Although it was mentioned earlier in this book in the introductory remarks about turtles in general and their histories, attention is called again to the gigantic *Archelon* illustrated on page 5. This huge skeleton was found in the Pierre Shale in South Dakota, which means that it is of Cretaceous age, and that the turtle lived and swam about in an ancient inland sea some seventy-five million years ago. The length of its shell is eleven feet, and there is a stretch of twelve feet between its front flippers. It had lost one of its rear limbs, probably to some voracious Mesozoic shark; but the end of the bone shows that healing had been successful, and that the accident had taken place several years before the animal died. In all probability these prehistoric reptiles were as tenacious of life as are their present-day descendants.

We have five species of sea turtles along our Atlantic shores. One is sought for its meat, one for its oil, one for the translucent beauty of its shell, and one is of little value except in a small measure for its oil. The fifth species is too uncommon to be of commercial value.

GREEN TURTLE

Chelonia mydas (Linne)

The green turtle, which gets its name from the greenish color of its fatty tissues, is the most highly prized of all our sea turtles as an article of food. It is a wide-ranging species, found in warm waters around the world. Our Atlantic form occurs along the coast from Florida to well down into South American waters, in the Mediterranean Sea, and along the West African coast. It was at one time moderately common as far north as Cape Hatteras, and even today an occasional specimen gets into the Gulf Stream and is found off the coast of Massachusetts during the late summer months. Specimens have even been reported from Newfoundland, but none have been captured there to prove their occurrence that far north. There are several old records of this turtle in Long Island Sound, including one "7 miles up" the Housatonic River (Linsley 1843). On the West Coast we find a very similar green turtle, but this Pacific form is recognized as a subspecies and is listed as *Chelonia mydas agassizi* Bocourt.

The shell is broad and low, highest in front, and is roughly heart-shaped when viewed from above. The surface is smooth, and its whole appearance is streamlined. The costal shields number four on each side (the loggerhead turtle, considered next, has five); and the marginal shields number about twenty-five, those at the rear making that end weakly serrate. The limbs have been modified into flippers, extremely efficient for swimming but clumsy for use on land. The front pair are especially large, and generally there is but a single nail on each "foot." The head is massive and armed with a strong and sharp beak. The turtle is completely unable to draw its flippers or its head into its shell for protection.

The carapace color is brownish olive, with wavy mottlings of darker hue. The plastron is white or yellowish white. The top of the head and the front parts of the limbs are marked by broad areas of brown separated by narrow lines of yellow in a reticulate pattern that reminds one of the markings on a giraffe. The throat and underparts are gray

Figure 38.   Green turtle.   (New York Zoological Society)

to yellowish gray. The largest specimen on record weighed 850 pounds and had a shell length of about five feet. Most of the green turtles seen in the market today range between fifty and two hundred pounds, and any individual with a shell four feet long and weighing in the neighborhood of five hundred pounds can be considered a truly gigantic specimen.

The green turtle is a vegetarian in the main; but under some conditions it is probably omnivorous, as captive specimens will usually feed upon fish without hesitation. It eats several kinds of marine plants, perhaps its favorite being

one that is popularly called "turtle grass" (*Zostera marina*).
This they chop off near the roots to obtain the fleshy and
tender part which alone is eaten, while the rest of the plant
floats to the surface and there collects in large drifts. This
is a sure indication that turtles are present and busy, and
one that has been taken advantage of by turtle hunters for
generations.

The ideal haunts of this species are in shallow, shoal
waters where there is an abundance of submerged plant life.
Among the keys and the cays of semitropical island chains
it finds numerous channels and bays to its liking. Green
turtles generally spend the daytime foraging over the submarine meadows and retire to deeper waters to spend the
nights. They are very fond of sleeping while floating at the
surface and apparently sleep quite soundly, for it is not hard
to row up to a slumbering individual and harpoon it.

They swim slowly and with solemn deliberation but with
considerable grace. Most of us will only have the opportunity of seeing them in action at some aquarium or marine
zoological studio; but as one drifts past with a measured
beat of its great forelimbs, the comparison to a lazy hawk
flopping along in the sky is quite marked. They appear to
have some degree of homing instinct, for specimens captured on the Dry Tortugas Islands and released on the Florida mainland have made their way back to those tiny specks
of land, more than a hundred miles away.

Nesting begins in the spring, at which time the female
comes ashore on some sandy beach, struggles clumsily inland
until well beyond the high-tide mark, and deposits from
seventy-five to three hundred eggs in an excavation she
laboriously scoops out in the sand. It is believed that a
mature turtle may lay three or four batches of eggs, at
intervals of about a month. After laying, the hole is covered up and rather well concealed, and Mrs. Turtle marches
back to the sea. She does, that is, if she is lucky, for it is
at this time that the green turtle is most vulnerable and is
relentlessly hunted. While the maternal instinct is so strong
she pays no attention to anything else; and a person can

walk right up to a specimen and turn it wrong-side up, thus rendering it helpless, and go on to the next one. Audubon relates an instance where one man took eight hundred turtles during a single season. One thing that probably is a big help to the turtles is that these egg-laying excursions almost always take place at night.

The eggs have also been gathered for food, and of course they represent buried treasure for any roaming raccoon or skunk. After the baby turtles hatch they have to negotiate that dangerous strip of sand between the nest and the water, toward which they unerringly head. They are forced to run a gauntlet of ravenous sea birds, only to meet with equally hungry fishes if they succeed in reaching the water. Only a small proportion of the little fellows are fortunate enough to survive and grow up.

From a commercial viewpoint, this is undoubtedly the most valuable reptile in the world. Despite the greenish hue of its fat, the flesh is red and very much like beefsteak in color and texture and, according to some epicures, in flavor as well. Captive specimens, such as those in markets, are kept on their backs. In water these turtles can easily right themselves when accidentally overturned, but on dry land they are completely helpless in this position. Seeing a row of green turtles, all on their backs in some market, makes one think of wanton cruelty; but it is a necessary practice unless the market can afford capacious tanks of sea water. The plastron is quite pliable and totally unable to support the great weight of an animal which is out of the water. It will support the turtle for the comparatively brief period of egg laying, but a specimen left in a normal position for any length of time has difficulty in breathing and soon dies.

The green turtle is ordinarily very mild mannered. An occasional specimen will bite; but most of them, even the big ones, can be handled quite safely. It goes without saying that any animal that has been hunted as extensively as this one will become scarce and hard to find. They are still taken in Florida waters and in the islands of the West Indies, but no specimens have been known to lay their eggs in this country for many years. The same is true in Bermuda, where they were once abundant, and in most of the famous nesting spots of years past. About the only places where they are known to nest regularly today are on Ascension Island in the South Atlantic and on various beaches along the Central American coast.

LOGGERHEAD TURTLE

Caretta caretta (Linne)

The loggerhead turtle is found along the Atlantic coast from Argentina to Nova Scotia and is well known in Europe and in the Mediterranean Sea, as well as along the west coast of Africa. Its home, of course, is in the warm seas of the tropics and semitropics; and its occurrence in places like Nova Scotia and Maine represents adventitious journeys

Figure 39.   Loggerhead turtle.   Photo by Isabelle Hunt Conant.

north in the mild waters of the Gulf Stream. Its center of abundance, with us, is in the Gulf of Mexico and the Florida Keys, where it is more abundant than the green turtle just described.

The loggerhead is shaped much like the green turtle, its shell elongate and heart shaped, with a relatively smooth surface in the adult stage. It differs in having a more massive head and in possessing five or more costal shields on each side of its carapace instead of four. The color above is reddish brown, the shields sometimes marbled with olive, while the plastron and underparts are yellowish gray. The head is covered above by large brownish shields, with paler areas between them; and the front flippers are decorated with hard scales along their forward edges. There are two nails on each foot, at least in young specimens. A really big loggerhead turtle today would have a shell about four feet long and would weigh between three and four hundred pounds. There are many records of examples brought ashore by fishermen all along our coast, with weights of seven or eight hundred pounds, and a few that went past the thousand-pound mark; but in all probability these extra-large individuals were the result of misidentification, and what the fishermen had harpooned and towed ashore were actually leatherback turtles.

Whereas the green turtle is predominantly vegetarian, the loggerhead is chiefly carnivorous. It undoubtedly consumes some plant material, but its main food consists of crabs, mollusks, fish, and other creatures of the sea, including sponges and jellyfish. Many a specimen has been hooked by some fisherman using shrimp or crab for bait, but it might be added that very few have been successfully brought to boat.

The loggerhead is more of a wandering turtle than the green turtle. This is probably correlated with food habits, as the green turtle can spend weeks on some submarine meadow while the loggerhead needs to move around in search of the food it lives upon. They are usually to be found in the deeper channels between islands and very commonly ascend rivers and streams for considerable distances, or until the water is no longer salty enough to suit them. They are frequently encountered miles at sea, where they are often observed floating at the surface, presumably sleeping. This species is much more likely to get into the Gulf Stream and wind up somewhere off the New England coast than is the green turtle.

This is the big turtle that comes ashore on Florida beaches in the spring and summer, usually on moonlight nights. A sandy beach is selected, and the turtle scrambles up to beyond the high-water line to excavate her nest. Fishermen recommend the first full moon in June as the best of all times to find them occupied with nesting activities. At the present time the loggerhead turtle nests on both coasts of Florida, in Georgia, and possibly South Carolina; but in the past it came ashore for egg laying all the way up to Virginia, which is the farthest north for any marine turtle.

The eggs are nearly round and are about an inch and a half in diameter. They have a soft but tough shell, and the number deposited in a nest averages about 130. Egg laying may take place two or three times during a season, and each year thousands of eggs are gathered for human use. They are reputed to be excellent when cooked in any number of ways (provided, of course, that they are fresh), and southern housewives used to declare that turtle eggs made the very best cakes. In spite of this practice of egg-gathering for so many years, the loggerhead continues to be fairly common in many localities and returns year after year to the same beaches and the same islands. While engaged in her maternal duty the female turtle is impervious to everything else and usually pays no attention whatever if a group of people are standing by, and even touching her. One man even reported holding his hat under a turtle and catching the eggs as they were laid!

The flesh of the loggerhead, about the consistency and color of beef, has often been described as "rank and unpalatable," but that is far from the truth. Granted that it is not as desirable as that of the green turtle, it is both tasty and nourishing, and while somewhat stringy and tough in the case of an old individual, makes first-rate stew or soup. It is a little hard to understand this "unpalatable" reputation when you consider that it has been eaten by thousands of people for hundreds of years.

The loggerhead is not mild in disposition, as the green turtle is; in fact, it is usually rather bad-tempered and will bite if it gets half a chance. Expert swimmers among the island natives have been known to enter the sea and capture green turtles by hand, even fairly large ones, but they know better than to tangle with a mature loggerhead in its native element. There is a case on record where five men in a rowboat tried to recapture a six-hundred-pound loggerhead that had escaped and was free in the shallow water of a small cove in Long Island Sound. They attempted to beat the reptile over the head with their oars, but one by one the turtle grasped and splintered the blades, and one man attempted to grab the shell and was badly bitten on the arm. They finally had to give up and return to shore with oars reduced to stumps and one wounded man. The turtle eventually got out into deeper water and the safety it richly deserved.

The form found in the Pacific and Indian oceans, and ranging from southern California to Chile on this side, is very much like our Atlantic loggerhead turtle but does differ enough to warrant a subspecific classification. It is properly listed as *Caretta caretta gigas* Deraniyagala.

HAWKSBILL TURTLE

Eretmochelys imbricata (Linne)

This is a smaller turtle, its maximum length being less than three feet. The record weight is 280 pounds, but most specimens are well under 100. The carapace is heart shaped, quite pointed behind, and not very much arched. The rear margins are saw toothed. Except in very old shells, there is a marked dorsal keel; and the vertebral shields as well as the costal overlap down the back, somewhat like the tiles of a roof, and hence the name *imbricata*.

The shields of the carapace are colored a "rich, warm, translucent yellow, dashed and spotted with rich brown tints" according to one writer of the last century. Actually, the translucent beauty of tortoise shell is not very evident in the living animal. It shows up best after the material has been thinned and polished, and then seen by transmitted light. The plastron is yellow. The fleshy parts of the turtle are dusky yellow below and reddish brown above, the dark patches sharply outlined with yellow. The flippers are well covered with small shields and are provided with two claws, or nails. The strongly hooked upper jaw gives the species its popular name of hawksbill turtle.

Figure 40.   Hawksbill turtle.   (New York Zoological Society)

Like the other marine turtles, this one is at home in warm seas. It is found in the Gulf of Mexico, all through the Caribbean Sea, and up the Atlantic coast to around South Carolina. It occurs in the Bahamas and in Bermuda, and occasional individuals drift north in the summer and are taken off the New England coast. The range of the hawksbill has been given as "from Massachusetts to Brazil," but its natural habitat is in warmer waters.

Although turtle shells have been used by man for many things, from ceremonial rattles and ornaments to cooking vessels, this is the only one that has a commercial value. Just as the green turtle has been hunted for its flesh, this one has been relentlessly pursued for its shell. The thirteen large shields of the carapace, five vertebral and eight costal shields, are the parts used. The marginal shields and the plastron have little value. A good-sized hawksbill will yield about eight pounds of tortoise shell. Few of the shields are large enough to be used for anything but smaller articles; but if they are heated in oil or boiled, they can be welded together under pressure and given any desired shape. In this manner artisans could produce sections of pure tortoise shell large enough to panel doors, although mostly it was (and is) used to inlay furniture and musical instruments and to serve as a veneer over small boxes, chests, etc. Even the scraps and dust can be pressed into combs, knife-handles, etc.

History is replete with accounts of man's cruelty to animals, particularly to gain some desired end, and the poor hawksbill has for ages been a martyr in this respect. If the shields are removed from an animal after death and decomposition has begun (and that occurs very quickly in the tropics), the color of the shell becomes clouded and milky. Natives on many tropical islands used to suspend the living turtle over a fire until the heat made the shields curl and loosen. After stripping its back, the unfortunate turtle was released in the sea, under the mistaken notion that it would "grow a new shell" and perhaps might be harvested again another year. Of course, nearly all of them died. More enlightened men have learned that you can get just as good results by first killing the turtle and then immersing it in boiling water. Various plastics can now be produced that equal tortoise shell in beauty and durability and can be made much cheaper. Hence, the demand for pure tortoise shell has fallen off to a large degree, and it seems probable that the hawksbill may find the future less hazardous than the past.

The hawksbill turtle will eat plants, but it very probably is chiefly carnivorous. Captive specimens thrive on fish and meat, and the list of animals known to provide food in the wild state includes worms, sea squirts, mollusks, crabs, and shrimps. They are reported to feed upon the Portuguese man-of-war and to close their eyes while so doing, thus avoiding the stinging tentacles.

The nesting habits of this species are about the same as those of the other marine turtles so far discussed. The female lays about 150 eggs at a time and probably nests at least twice in a season. The eggs are about an inch and a half in diameter. Sandy or gravelly beaches on islands are most frequently utilized and, like the others, these inland treks take place at night.

The hawksbill is generally regarded as an irascible turtle, ready and willing to bite at any hand or foot within reach; and the sharp beak can inflict a painful, tearing wound. It should be emphasized, however, that this refers to turtles that are harassed or tormented. The hawksbill turtle never attacks swimmers or otherwise bothers anything that is not bothering him.

This is another species whose flesh is often described as of poor quality, yet it is eaten in many parts of its range; and some experimenters declare it is excellent provided the turtle in question is a young one. The eggs are eagerly gathered in some localities and eaten either fresh or cured. The Central American natives sometimes boil, shell, and dry them, and string them like beads, to be smoked for future use. However, the chief value of this species lies in the decorative possibilities of its multishaded, horny carapace.

The hawksbill turtle of the Pacific and Indian oceans differs slightly and constantly from the one we are familiar with on the Atlantic coast. It is recognized as a subspecies, and has been named *Eretmochelys imbricata squamata* Agassiz. Its habits are the same as those of our hawksbill; and it has been extensively persecuted for its shell for a much longer period of time, as specimens from the shores of Asia were hung up and roasted alive long before our Caribbean area was discovered.

RIDLEY TURTLE

Lepidochelys kempi (Garman)

The Ridley turtle is probably the smallest of the marine turtles, rarely exceeding a couple of feet in length, its maximum apparently less than three. It looks considerably like a small loggerhead and is commonly mistaken for one. But its shell is more heart shaped and broad in relation to its length; the whole animal appears more chunky and heavy in proportion to its size, and there are several anatomical characteristics that are different. Perhaps the most evident difference is its color, which is always predominantly gray. The carapace bears three spiny longitudinal ridges, very prominent in young specimens but rather obscure in adults.

There is a common belief among Southern fishermen that this turtle is a cross between a loggerhead and a hawksbill turtle, and it bears many local names that suggest this partnership, such as "hybrid turtle," "bastard turtle," and "mulatto turtle." It is, however, a perfectly good genus, quite different from either the hawksbill or the loggerhead turtles.

The Ridley turtle has a somewhat restricted range, its chief haunts being in the northern sections of the Gulf of Mexico. It is seen occasionally in southern Florida, and individuals are taken sporadically in northern waters up to southern New England. Following the warm summer currents, some are swept overseas; and the Ridley occasionally turns up on European and African shores. It appears to be absent from the Bahamas and the West Indies.

The Ridley turtle seems to prefer shallow water around mangrove lagoons but may be seen several miles at sea. Its food is made up chiefly of crabs, shrimps, and mollusks, with probably a small amount of plant material. Opinions vary as to the flavor of its flesh. Apparently young specimens are not bad eating; in fact they are sometimes marketed as "chicken ridleys," but when older their flesh is commonly regarded as inferior to either the green or loggerhead turtles.

One thing generally agreed upon by all who have observed this species at close range is that it has the most nasty temper of any marine species. The Ridley turtle is reputed to exhibit almost hysterical rage when caught, thrashing about and snapping at everything within reach.

LEATHERBACK TURTLE

Dermochelys coriacea (Linne)

This is by far the largest of the living turtles and the most completely adapted for aquatic life. It is unique among turtles in that the vertebrae and ribs are not fused with the carapace but are free within it. In fact, this reptile is so structurally different that it is placed in a family by itself (Dermochelidae) of which it is the only species. Some authorities regard it as a direct descendant of the Cretaceous *Archelon.*

Various popular names applied to this marine giant are "leathery turtle," "luth," "harp turtle," "lyre turtle," and "blubber turtle." Its shell length may be as much as seven feet; and while several published accounts of "nearly a ton" are open to question, there is no doubt about its reaching a weight of more than one thousand pounds.

The shell is like a big box, the dorsal and ventral halves being directly continuous, forming an unbroken case all around. It is composed of a mosaic of hundreds of bony plates, embedded and covered by a tough, leathery skin. The upper surface bears seven longitudinal ridges that converge at the tail end of the shell, with wide concave furrows between them. There are five less prominent ridges on the lower side. The limbs are converted into flattened paddles, which are completely destitute of nails and are also without scales, being smooth like the flippers of a seal. The head, which is covered with small plates, is remarkable for its rela-

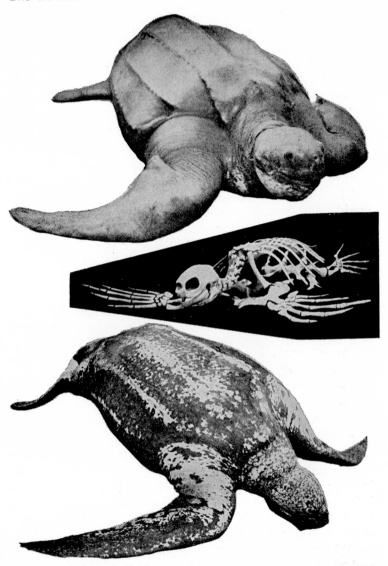

Figure 41. Male leatherback turtle taken off Montauk Point, New York, in June 1951. Its weight was 1100 pounds and the spread between flippers, 8 feet. The lower picture shows the underside, and the middle picture shows the skeleton.

tively large size and globose form. The sharply hooked beak has two triangular cusps situated between three deep notches. The neck is not retractible.

The color is dark greenish black above, sometimes with a few yellowish marks but more often uniform in tone. The underside is usually mottled and spotted with grayish white, and this mottling or speckling continues on the lower surfaces of the limbs and on the neck right up to the chin. Very young individuals are much more brightly marked than are the oldsters, but partly grown specimens are practically never seen.

The leatherback is found in warm seas all around the world. Our Atlantic variety is most at home in the Caribbean Sea but occurs commonly in the Gulf of Mexico, along the east coast of Florida, and in the Bahamas. Because it is more given to wandering in the sea than any other marine turtle, it very often gets into the Gulf Stream and travels north. It has been taken in Nova Scotian waters, and there are many records of its occurrence off the coasts of Maine and Massachusetts. To the south it wanders as far as Argentina, and on the other side of the Atlantic it is known from the British Isles to South Africa. The form found in the Pacific and Indian oceans is known as *Dermochelys coriacea schlegeli* (Garman).

Despite its huge bulk, the leatherback turtle is extremely graceful in the water, diving and turning with the greatest of ease. The fact that juvenile specimens are almost never seen, once they get past the hatchling stage, suggests that they spend all of their time at sea; and only the adults come in near shore. They are probably omnivorous in feeding habits, as both plant and animal material have been found in their stomachs. That they are capable of taking care of themselves in the water is well attested by more than one small-boat party—the turtle resisting capture by using its jaws and its flippers with telling effect, and all the while emitting various grunts, bellows, and roars. It is believed, however, that most of its vocal efforts are produced by expelling air.

Most of those which are brought back to shore are harpooned from larger vessels.

The leatherback turtle nests like the others. The female comes ashore and deposits 150 or more eggs in a pit that she excavates well back of the high-water mark. They probably nest on the Florida mainland on rare occasions, possibly in the wilder regions, but most of them lay their eggs on smaller islands throughout the Caribbean area and always at night. The eggs are spherical, nearly two inches across, and are covered by a thin, flexible shell.

Although the eggs are eaten by natives when found, the nests are so infrequent that they are not an important source of food. In fact, to find a nesting leatherback is a once-in-a-lifetime event for any herpetologist. The flesh is generally considered unfit for human food, as it is too oily. The turtles used to be sought for their oil, a square foot of the blubbery layer beneath the skin yielding about one pint of oil.

2

THE LIZARDS

THE LIZARDS form a large and interesting group, ranging from ten-foot monsters with claws longer than those of a leopard and capable of overpowering and devouring a small deer to tiny limbless, eyeless, wormlike creatures that spend most of their lives underground. Included, too, are examples that swim as expertly as the crocodilians, some that can run head downward on horizontal surfaces, and others that sail from tree to tree after the manner of a flying squirrel.

Like the turtles, their history goes back millions of years; but they are not as ancient as the turtles are. There were many lizard-like creatures during the latter part of the Paleozoic Era, and by the end of the Permian Period many of the principal lines of evolution had been established. The evidence for this belief is partly direct, through the Permian fossil record, and partly indirect, based upon the presence in overlying Triassic rocks of groups which must have had a long antecedent development. The first true lizards appeared during the next, or Jurassic, period well over 100 million years ago.

The typical lizard has fore and hind limbs (although either pair, or both, may be absent) and a long, whiplike tail that is easily broken. The body is covered with scales, mostly rather fine but sometimes large and horny or even spiny. Unlike the snakes, to which they are rather closely related, the lizard has a nonexpansible mouth; and its teeth are fused to the jaw instead of set in sockets. Also unlike the snake, most (but not all) lizards have movable eyelids and external ear openings. The scales on the belly are small and numerous, in place of the broad scutes of the serpents.

It is uncertain just what may be the world's smallest lizard, but there is no doubt about which is the largest. The Komodo Monitor, or Komodo Dragon *Varanus komodoensis* Ouwens, rivals the crocodiles in size, growing to a length of ten feet and attaining a weight in excess of 300 pounds. It is far larger and heavier than any other known lizard and is found in the Sunda Islands, a chain in the Malay Archipelago. It is a heavy-bodied, carnivorous reptile with a long, strongly muscled tail; a rather massive head; and a long, darting, forked tongue. In captivity this colossal lizard is reported as docile and mild mannered, but in its native haunts the Komodo Monitor could very well be a dangerous adversary.

By far the greater proportion of the lizards, including all of the big fellows, are confined to the warmer portions of the globe, only a limited number of species occurring in temperate latitudes. The vast majority of these are small creatures, lightning quick in movement, and very much opposed to being caught.

Many of the lizards do well in captivity, notably the American "chameleon" (*Anolis*), the horned lizards, the gila monster, and most of the skinks. Some of the others are difficult to maintain in good health, but with proper care nearly all of them may be kept for considerable periods.

Most lizards are sun-loving reptiles, but it is a mistake to believe that you have to keep them in bright sunlight every day and all day. As a matter of fact, they get along very well when kept indoors with no sun at all. The main requirement is a dry and well-ventilated cage, and of course during cold weather you must see that the temperature does not fall much below 70 degrees. Give them a few inches of sand and gravel to dig in, flat stones and bark to hide under,

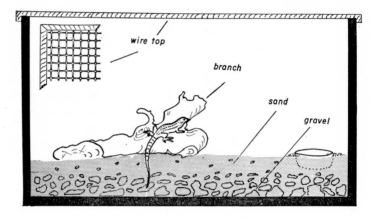

Figure 42. Basic cage for lizards.

and a gnarled branch to climb, and they will be quite content. Keep a small dish of clean water in the cage at all
times. Lizards don't drink very often, and some of them
never do learn to take water from a dish. The little *Anolis*,
for example, gets its moisture early in the morning from
drops of dew on the foliage; and a specimen in captivity may
die of thirst with a pan of water close by. For these finicky
species, sprinkle water generously over a spray of leaves; and
put it in the cage first thing in the morning.

Many times throughout the pages of this book, particularly in the lizard section, the reader will come across the
name "mealworms" in reference to food for captive animals.
In the summertime one can generally keep his pets well fed
with no great trouble. The fields and meadows are rich in
insect life; and by sweeping a net back and forth in the tall
grass you will come up with all sorts of flies, ants, beetles,
grasshoppers, crickets, spiders, etc. Flies, millers, and ants
may be trapped in a wire box with some sweet substance like
honey or molasses; grubs and caterpillers can be found with
little exertion; and a host of "bugs" may be collected at night
around outdoor lights. All in all, your specimens can be kept
well supplied with food at this time of the year with comparative ease. The winter months, however, do present a

problem. If you live in the northern part of the country, insects cease to be available by December at the latest, and from then until late April the only insects you can feed your lizards are the ones you raise yourself. Mealworms are the easiest and cheapest to rear, and a box or two containing colonies will tide you over the frigid months until warm weather brings another fresh supply of insects and larvae in the woods and fields.

Of the many different kinds of insects found in stored grains and cereals, the mealworms are the most easily recognized. They are world-wide in distribution and are easily obtained. Many dealers in animal supplies advertise them at a dollar or less for three hundred. There are two species common in this country: the so-called yellow mealworm, *Tenebrio moliter* and the brown mealworm, *Tenebrio obscurus*. The adult beetles of the two species look much alike; the former is shiny brown to black, and the latter is dull pitchy black. Both are about three-fourths of an inch long.

The females are prolific egg layers, depositing three or four hundred eggs when mature, after which they die. The larvae are about one inch long when fully grown, yellowish tan in color, and about an eighth of an inch in diameter. They grow quite rapidly, reaching full size in about three months. They molt, or cast their skins, many times during this growth. They do not spin a cocoon; but when ready to pupate there is a final shedding of the skin, and underneath is a chrysalid. The mealworm undergoes a dormant period while in this stage. The pupa, about three-fourths of an inch long, is whitish in color at first but turns yellow in a few days. In warm weather the adult beetle may emerge in a week. By keeping your mealworms in a moderately cool spot, you can prolong the larval, or "worm" stage, sometimes for months; and that is the stage your lizards are interested in.

With proper precautions mealworms can be raised with little effort or attention. Prepare a wooden box about two feet long by a foot wide and six inches deep. The top can be a sheet of tin, wallboard, or plywood, just so it provides a cover. It should be cut so it fits loosely on a narrow wooden strip tacked all around the inside of the box, just below the rim.

Fill your box a little more than half full of some cereal for the mealworms to live in and to eat. Most growers use wheat bran to which they add a little commercial meat scrap, about one part meat scrap to twenty parts bran. Oatmeal will do just about as well. Start the culture with about three hundred mealworms, allow them to develop into beetles and lay eggs, and you are in business.

It is a good plan to prepare three boxes; and as soon as you have a supply of pupae, distribute some in all three. Then, when all three colonies are progressing nicely, you can feed your lizards mealworms from one or two and always have a third box of larvae left to develop into adults to carry on the supply.

Mealworms like moist foodstuffs, so from time to time add potato peelings, apple slices, or lettuce. Occasionally a slice of bread, slightly moistened, may be added. Do not mix these with the bran, but place them on a square of cardboard that can be discarded later on. You must not allow the bran to get too moist or molds or fungus may develop and ruin the culture. Add fresh bran as needed.

THE GECKOS

Geckos, of which there are hundreds of species distributed over the warmer parts of the globe, are distinctive little lizards, easily recognized. Unfortunately, they are not common in this country and are confined to the most southern sections. They are small creatures with a relatively soft skin with tiny scales, a short, plump body, and sturdy limbs. The head is somewhat flattened as a rule. The great majority have the digits modified for climbing, either with the fingers and toes expanded or swollen into pads at their tips. There is no sticky substance involved, but numerous tiny ridges on the "pad" produce a suction that enables the lizard to run

up a sheer wall, even a pane of glass, and to travel upside
down on a rough ceiling.

Mostly, they are nocturnal. They have big eyes with
vertical pupils, and in all but a few species there are no eyelids. The tail is thick but very fragile and easily broken
off, a trick that allows many a gecko to escape from an
enemy. A new tail is soon regenerated. Most, possibly all,
of the geckos have a voice, rather feeble in many cases and
sounding like a soft click or chirp. Some imagine the sound
resembles "gecko," and hence the name. They are all insectivorous, and many of them show a decided preference
for living in human habitations.

Few creatures have given rise to a greater amount of
fable and legend than the geckos. Such legends are probably due to the nocturnal and domestic habits of these
animals, their uncanny ability to walk upside down on ceil-
ings, their dilated toes, and their general appearance. In
many countries they are feared as much or even more than
the most poisonous snake. They are believed to eject venom
from their toes, their bite is certain death, and anything they
have walked across will be poisoned. In southern Spain,
where they are abundant about houses, the natives call them
"osga" and consider them terribly dangerous creatures; and
in Egypt one rather common species was popularly known
as the "father of leprosy."

Actually, of course, all geckos are absolutely harmless.
They are far too weak to even scratch the skin if they were
to bite (and they almost never do), and they have no
venomous powers at all. They tame very easily, do well in
captivity, and make excellent pets.

YELLOW-HEADED GECKO

Gonatodes fuscus (Hallowell)

This little fellow is an inhabitant of Cuba, Jamaica, and
Central and South America. It has been introduced into
Florida and is now to be found in the vicinity of Key West.

Authorities believe that its true home is from Nicaragua
south and that those in the West Indies are also the result
of introduction.

It is a slender lizard about three inches from the tip of its
nose to the end of its tail, and the last half of this is tail. Its
hind legs are more robust than the front ones, and the toes
lack the expanded pads that are so characteristic of most of
the geckos; in fact, the group to which this reptile belongs is
known as the "padless geckos." The head is proportionally
large; the neck quite thick; and the eyes are very large and
lidless, the pupil vertical by day and round after dark. The
lizard's scales are small and beadlike and somewhat translucent.

The head and neck are yellow, sometimes yellowish
orange, with the rest of the animal some shade of gray.
There may be a tinge of brown, and it may be uniform in
tone or there may be spots and blotches of darker hue. There
is frequently a whitish line at the neck, particularly noticeable in dark-colored specimens; and the sides are commonly
dotted with black. The underside is pale gray.

This gecko is said to be more active in the daytime than
most of its tribe. It is generally found around old abandoned
buildings and shacks. Despite its "padless" feet, it is quite
capable of running up the side of a wall, although it is a
trusting sort of creature and usually not very hard to catch.
It lays from eight to ten white, brittle-shelled eggs, commonly in some rotting crevice of a building or under a pile
of debris.

MEDITERRANEAN GECKO

Hemidactylus turcicus (Linne)

This is a world traveler if there ever was one, and it seems
strange that such a tiny and delicate creature could have
obtained a foothold in so many parts of the world. It occurs
along the shores of the Mediterranean and Red seas, in
southern Portugal and Spain, the Canary Islands, and in

Egypt, Morocco, Turkey, and so on all the way to Iran and
the Persian Gulf. On our side of the globe it is found in the
West Indies and in southern Florida. It is often called the
Turkish gecko or the warty gecko.

The over-all length is about four inches, the sturdy tail
making up nearly half. The limbs are rather well developed,
and the head is large and somewhat flattened. The eyes are
quite large, with vertical pupils; and there are no lids. The

Figure 43. Mediterranean gecko.

fingers and toes, five on each foot, are provided with tiny
claws and are expanded or dilated so that the lizard can run
over perpendicular surfaces with considerable agility. The
upper surface is covered with minute granules, mixed with
larger tubercles, so that the creature's back, all the way down
on the tail, is indeed "warty." There is a tiny ear-opening
just back of, and below, the eye.

The color above varies from gray to almost white, with
the head and back well spotted with darker blotches that
may be large and irregular or small and roundish. If the
ground color is gray there may be several whitish dots along
the sides. The tail is more or less banded by broken bars
of a darker shade; and the limbs, even the digits, are likely
to be banded or spotted. The underside is whitish or yel-

lowish. As with many of the geckos, the colors are curiously translucent, and one writer states that during the nesting season the white eggs shimmer through the body in certain lights. There is some ability to change color, and a specimen may be quite dark during the day and a ghostly grayish white at night.

In Florida this species is established in the Keys, especially around Key West, and it has been taken repeatedly near the city of Miami. It appears to be confined almost wholly to human habitations and occurs in occupied houses as well as abandoned buildings. Unless disturbed, they are not to be seen in the daytime; but after dark they come forth from their hiding places in cracks and crevices and under loose boards and scamper about over the walls in search of insects. In some localities, particularly in the West Indies, the natives regard them with something akin to horror, for they are convinced that they are deadly poisonous. Of course they are completely harmless, and actually they do a pretty good job of keeping down the ant and fly populations in any building where they take up residence.

Around Key West they seem to be observed most often at night, on the window screens of lighted porches or rooms. Here they feast upon the insects that are attracted by the light. The geckos do not appear to mind the brightly illuminated screen, even though they shun light during the daytime.

ASHY GECKO

Sphaerodactylus cinereus Wagler

The ashy gecko is found at Key West and Key Largo in Florida. It is probably another importation from the West Indies, where it is relatively common. The length is about three inches; and its build is rather slender, the head somewhat flattened with the snout drawn out to a point. It is covered with tiny scales that are weakly keeled. Each finger

and toe ends in a swollen pad, with a tiny claw at one side
that is partially covered by a sheath of skin. The eyes are
large, and the pupils are vertical like those of a cat. There
is a small black spine above each eye, and the ear-openings
are minute.

The color on the back is grayish or reddish brown, with
small pale yellowish specks scattered more or less regularly
over the whole surface, including the limbs and tail. There
may be a lining up of these spots on the head to form longitudinal lines, and a few short bars may be present in the
vicinity of the neck. The lower surface is uniform pale
brown. Juvenile specimens exhibit transverse bars of reddish brown on their backs; in fact, the young appear so different from their parents that they were once considered a
separate species and were given the name of *Sphaerodactylus
elegans* MacLeay.

This gecko appears to be almost exclusively nocturnal; at
least it is very rarely to be seen during the day. It may be
found about buildings, on lumber piles in the woods, and
around the old boarded cisterns on the Keys. It is occasionally attracted to some lighted screen door or window,
but it is far from common in this country. Like the other
geckos, this one can run about over smooth walls with con-
sumate skill. Carr states that it lays its eggs, white and
brittle-shelled, in rock piles and in trash heaps.

REEF GECKO

Sphaerodactylus notatus Baird

This is a really little fellow, the smallest gecko in this country, its over-all length generally less than three inches. Its
home is in Cuba and the Bahamas; but it has become established in extreme southern Florida, where it may be found
on many of the Keys as well as on the mainland. It is a
ruggedly built lizard, despite its diminutive size, with sturdy
limbs, a somewhat thickened tail, and a pointed head that

is slightly flattened. The eyes are without lids, and the pupils are vertical. The tips of its digits are swollen into efficient suction pads.

The colors are rather constant, but the pattern is somewhat variable. The ground color is grayish brown, generally quite pale; and the entire upper surface may be speckled with small, round, dark spots; or the spots may be so distributed as to produce longitudinal lines which tend to form dark stripes on the head and neck. The underside is yellowish gray, the throat commonly showing scattered black dots. Some examples display a pattern that is a sort of combination of stripes and spots, and with others there may be no dark markings above at all.

The reef gecko is probably the most common of the geckos in southeastern United States, and in certain localities it might even be described as abundant. Carr states that it is possible to find twenty or more on the walls of a single cistern. They occur in hardwood hammocks, in dry woods, and stony places in general, and are even collected occasionally in the tangles of driftwood just back from open beaches. Like most of its tribe, the reef gecko is not averse to taking up residence in old wooden buildings.

LEAF-FOOTED GECKO

Phyllodactylus tuberculosus Wiegmann

Sometimes called the tubercular gecko, this distinctive species belongs in Mexico, living throughout the length of Lower (or Baja) California. It is entitled to be listed as a United States lizard by virtue of the fact that its northern range extends just above the border into extreme southern California. As a matter of fact, this one and the next two species to be described (the latter known as ground geckos) are the only real natives we have, as all of the Florida geckos are immigrants.

This species gets to be about five inches long, with the tail making up a little more than half, provided it is in good shape. The tail is very feebly connected to the body and is cast off unhesitatingly when the lizard is in a tight situation. The new tail is seldom as long as the original, and it is a bit unusual to find specimens with perfect tails. The body is rather slender and the limbs relatively long and sturdy. The head is large, the prominent eyes lidless and with vertical pupils. The scales on the back are keeled. The digits all end in a double flattish pad, with a tiny claw visible between the two parts. As the name tubercular would imply, there are numerous warty tubercles scattered over the dorsal surface, and in certain lights the lizard appears somewhat translucent.

The general ground color of this gecko is very pale gray, sometimes with a yellowish cast. There is a pattern of dark gray or black transverse bars on the back and tail; but these bars are most irregular and frequently broken, so that the dorsal surface may be more spotted than barred. There is usually a conspicuous dark line along the side of the head, passing through the eye. The limbs and feet are more or less spotted or marbled with dark gray; and the underside is white, sometimes with tiny brown dots.

"Leaf-footed" is not a bad name for these lizards, as the curious double flat pads on each finger and toe do suggest paired leaves. The name *Phyllodactylus* means "leaf fingered." These geckos live in rocky or stony country, commonly on some arid hillside, and they are quite expert in running up the sheer face of a boulder. They are nocturnal in habits, spending the daytime hiding away in a crack or crevice among the rocks and coming out after dark to hunt for night-prowling insects.

DESERT BANDED GECKO

Coleonyx variegatus (Baird)

This is a ground gecko and, together with the next species, is most ungecko-like in appearance. The toes terminate in tiny nails, with no swellings or pads at all, and the eyes are equipped with eyelids.

The desert banded gecko occurs in southern California, the southern tips of Utah and Nevada, throughout most of Arizona, and on down into Mexico. It is a slender and elongate lizard, five or six inches in length, the tail thickened and robust but the limbs relatively thin and puny. There are five fingers and five toes, all without the slightest evidence of any suction pads. The head is proportionally large, with big eyes that have vertical pupils. The skin appears more granular than it does scaly, although small overlapping scales are present.

Figure 44.   Desert banded gecko.

The color above is yellowish gray, with broad transverse bands of brown which continue as bars on the tail. Each band has a paler area at its center. Juvenile specimens are strongly and regularly banded with the two colors; but older examples are likely to have the bands broken into irregular lines, generally with additional spots between the bands. The head is yellowish gray, well spotted with brown, and the limbs are similarly marked. The underside is white, with the bottom of the tail frequently yellowish.

This little lizard is at home in rocky desert hills, among the mesquite and the cactus. They are nocturnal in habits and are not ordinarily seen abroad during the daylight hours. The skin is exceedingly tender, and it is probable that they are unable to endure the bright sun for any length of time. They feed upon spiders, ground beetles, ants, and various other small insects, and hide away under flat stones or in crevices long before the desert sands are heated by another day. Walking slowly along some desert road after dark, and sweeping the rays of your searchlight back and forth over the surrounding terrain, sometimes results in the capture of several of these interesting lizards.

When alarmed, the desert banded gecko often runs with its tail curled up over its back; and if really frightened it may face its tormenter and rise up on stiff legs, its tail and head both elevated. The pose is a bit ridiculous, for the gecko is totally incapable of defending itself, even against another lizard the same size. If handled it usually protests, with a squeaking sound. It tames very easily, however, and makes a good pet, although its activities will be pretty much confined to the hours after dark.

TEXAS BANDED GECKO

Coleonyx brevis Stejneger

The Texas banded gecko, as its name implies, comes from the Lone Star state. It occurs in the southwestern sections of Texas, in southeastern New Mexico, and ranges south into Old Mexico as well. Its distribution is well separated from that of *variegatus* just described. It is a smaller lizard, averaging about four inches from nose to tail-tip. Like the ground gecko of farther west, this one has eyelids; and there are no pads on the ends of its digits.

The colors are about the same as those of the desert

Figure 45.   Texas banded gecko.

banded gecko, a pale yellowish gray or fawn color; but the
crossing bands are proportionally wider. Young specimens
are very boldly banded, the brown almost double the width
of the fawn color; and the rather large head is heavily
spotted. As the animal grows, the brown bars become
broken into blotches; and adult specimens frequently have
their backs so marbled that only a trace of the banding remains.

This gecko shows a preference for rocky places, rather
than the sandy wastes of the open desert. It occurs in
canyons and in foothills, where it can be sure of finding
plenty of rocks to hide under and between. It is nocturnal,
doing its prowling after dark, and during the day may often
be found by overturning stones or prying apart slabs of thin-
bedded rock.

The Texas banded gecko, sometimes known as the lesser
ground gecko, is easily tamed and does quite well in captivity, living contentedly on a diet of flies, mealworms, and
other small insects. It needs to be kept in a dry and warm
(but not too hot) terrarium, and like most of its group it will
be most active after sundown.

CAROLINA ANOLE

Anolis carolinensis Voigt

This is the so-called "American Chameleon," a common little lizard in our Southland. It occurs throughout Florida, north to North Carolina, and west through the Gulf states all the way through Texas to the Rio Grande. The true chameleons are prehensile-tailed lizards, and are confined to the Old World, but this species goes through such rapid color changes it is small wonder that the name has been applied to them. This is the little lizard that used to be sold at circuses, country fairs, and carnivals a few years ago, each one with a short piece of string fastened around its neck

Figure 46. Carolina anole.

with a safety pin so that the animal could be pinned to one's lapel. Humane laws have outlawed this practice in most of our states. We have but the one species native to this country, along with a couple that have been introduced; but the genus *Anolis* is actually the largest of the whole lizard clan, with hundreds of species in tropic lands. In Haiti, for example, there are no less than twenty-seven species recognized, in addition to several subspecies.

The Carolina anole is a slender lizard, attaining a length of nearly seven inches, of which the long tail constitutes about two-thirds. Most specimens are about five inches long. The head is elongate, somewhat flattened, and wedge-shaped, with a ridgelike process on the forehead, shaped something like a spearhead and pointing toward the nose. The body is covered with tiny scales; and the skin is rather loose fitting, particularly around the neck where it hangs in a loose fold at the throat. In males this fold is often spread fan-wise.

The limbs are long and graceful, and each is terminated with five slender digits. The toes and all but the first finger on each "hand" are swollen, or expanded, near their tips, with the last joint and a long nail projecting beyond the swollen part. These miniature "pads" are covered with parallel ridges, enabling the anole to scurry about on all sorts of surfaces and in all positions. The tail is round in cross section.

The well-known ability to alter its color has earned this lizard the popular name of "chameleon," by which (along with "green lizard" and "fence lizard") it is known throughout its range. Low temperatures generally induce a dark color, and high temperatures a lighter shade. The commonest color for this anole is pale green, or greenish gray. If excited, as when frightened or engaged in fighting, the creature turns a bright emerald green; and when resting it is generally a deep gray or brown. Contrary to popular opinion, the color of its surroundings is no guarantee of the lizard's color; and a bright green specimen may often be seen on a gray rock, while a dull brown individual climbs about among the green leaves.

The story is told of an enterprising merchant who displayed a half-dozen specimens in his show window, on a background of four different squares of color. The amusing result was that the lizards huddled together on the green square and all became dull brown!

Dark specimens usually show darker streaks on the sides of the throat; and a white or yellowish stripe is present along the sides of the head, just below the eye. The loose skin on the throat of the male, commonly called the "dewlap," may be red or orange and becomes very bright when it is spread, as it is during courtship. After death the body is usually dull green with scattered blotches of black. Specimens in alcohol turn gray.

The Carolina anole is an active, sun-loving reptile, strictly diurnal in habits, that will often be seen scampering along fence rails, over rocks, or among the foliage of trees. They are perfectly at home in shrubs, vines, and other vegetation both high and low, and about old buildings. They appear nervous and uneasy on the ground, and are thoroughly arboreal by choice, and have been observed at the tops of tall trees. They are not averse to water, and if alarmed on a branch that overhangs a pond they do not hesitate to jump into the water and swim away.

They begin their activities by mid-morning and are on the go all during the day. At night they sleep in exposed positions, clinging tightly to branches or weed stems. They show an affinity for water and are most numerous about the borders of ponds and marshes, although it may well be that their food is more plentiful in such places. In Florida they do not hibernate. They may be inactive during cool spells but are out and around whenever it is warm enough.

They feed exclusively upon insects, which they are expert in stalking, and sometimes enter houses to scurry over the walls in search of flies and mosquitoes. Among the branches they are sure-footed little sprites, darting about like tiny green squirrels, and often leap several inches in order to catch some luckless fly. Surely no tree frog is more at home in the tree tops than this little anole.

During courtship time the males engage in much fighting. Two of them will face each other and dip and bob, both turning a brilliant green and spreading their throat fans to the utmost. Then they rush at each other and scramble furiously for a brief period, until one decides he has had enough and beats a hasty retreat. The victor then struts around pompously in his rich green uniform. In June or July, the female lays two eggs, buried in loose soil and generally in damp places. The eggs are oval, about one-half inch long, grayish white in color, and have soft shells. They hatch in about six weeks.

Probably more of these lizards have been taken home for pets than any other American species. This is partly because of their abundance and the comparative ease of capture, and also because they are commonly sold in the South from souvenir stands for a small price, usually no more than fifty cents apiece. Unfortunately, most of them do not survive very long in captivity, although they will do quite well if properly cared for. Many youngsters try to feed them on a mixture of sugar and water, or on bread and milk, and their pets soon die. The anole insists on living insects and will eat nothing else. Give it mealworms or flies (it will not accept earthworms), and it will soon learn to take them from your fingers. It is accustomed to getting its drinking water by lapping up dewdrops from foliage in the early morning, and it is a known fact that most anoles will die of thirst with a pan of water in their cage. Try sprinkling a little water over the leaves early each day, and your pets should get along fine. Some have lived in captivity for three years.

In the Key West region of Florida a West Indies species has been introduced. It is called the Key West anole, *Anolis stejnegeri*. The Cuban brown anole is said to have obtained a foothold in the vicinity of Tampa, Florida. Its scientific name is *Anolis sagrei*. Both are quite like our native anole, and when seen in the trees it is not easy to tell them apart.

DESERT IGUANA

Dipsosaurus dorsalis (Baird and Girard)

This attractive lizard is also known as the keel-backed lizard and the crested lizard. Its home is in the arid Southwest, from southern California and Nevada south through

Figure 47. Desert iguana.

western Arizona into Mexico. It is a well-built, stocky creature, its over-all length about fifteen inches, and its body
length between five and six inches. The limbs are sturdy,
the toes long and slender, the tail stout and tapering, and
the head is rather small and blunt. There is a series of
raised, strongly keeled, somewhat enlarged scales on the
lizard's back, forming a sort of ridge extending from just
back of the head to part way down the tail. This characteristic corresponds to the well-known dorsal fringe of the
iguanas, tropical lizards to which this species is closely
allied.

The desert iguana is pale gray in color, its back well
dotted with light reddish brown reticulations that become
slate colored on the sides. The dots are often so arranged
that they form longitudinal lines on the sides. The limbs
are decorated with darker spotted bands, while the upper
surface of the tail bears half-rings of small rounded dots.
Males have a patch of orange brown on each side of the tail.
The creature's predominant gray shades seem to adapt it
perfectly to the sands on which it lives and is usually seen.
The head is gray, a little darker on top, with a few obscure
bars around the lips. The eyes are moderately large, and
the ear-openings are particularly evident.

This species is a lover of flat, sandy desert country, being most active earlier in the morning and later in the afternoon. It escapes the scorching midday periods by resting in rodent burrows or in the scant shade of some cactus or scrubby bush. It is a very wary lizard and hard to catch, but at the same time it appears to be a curious animal and will often prop itself high on its front legs, where, with its head held ridiculously up in the air, it will stare intently at you until it decides you are getting a little too close for comfort. It is an exceedingly fast runner when it does take off and sometimes rises up on its hind legs and goes dashing away like a miniature dinosaur. If an escaping specimen manages to get wedged in a rocky crevice it will inflate its body, like a chuckwalla, so that it is difficult to draw it out without injury.

The desert iguana is listed as a vegetarian, feeding almost exclusively upon various desert plants, blossoms, and fruits. It will eat some insects and has been observed swallowing a small lizard. It has been estimated that 87 per cent of its food is plant material; but in captivity the story is somewhat different, at least with an individual currently in the author's possession. This example, some ten inches long, steadfastedly refuses to eat any vegetable material offered, although it has been tried with lettuce, cabbage, tomato, melon, berries, banana, apple slices, pears, and several other items. It will, however, greedily devour any caterpillar, mealworm, or other insect as fast as it is dropped into its cage. This perhaps points up the fact that we should not describe a creature's habits in a wild state by what it may do under the artificial conditions of captivity.

CHUCKWALLA

Sauromalus obesus (Baird)

With the exception of the Gila Monster, this is the largest and heaviest lizard likely to be observed in this country. Fully grown adults may attain a length of close to seventeen inches and a weight of three or four pounds, but the average specimen encountered is apt to be between ten and twelve inches long. It is a creature of hot and dry canyons and may be found from southern California to Arizona and north to southern Utah and Nevada, rather commonly in some localities. In California it is sometimes called "Alderman's Lizard."

The chuckwalla is quite stout, as its specific name *obesus* indicates. It has a husky body and a thick, blunt, heavy tail. The limbs are heavy and stubby, with claws that are thick and strong and certainly not intended for speedy traveling. There is a prominent fold of skin at the neck; and just behind the jawbones, on each side of the face, are a pair of short, hornlike projections. The scales are quite small in relation to the reptile's size. The skin usually appears too big for the animal and develops loose folds and heavy wrinkles along the sides.

Young or partially grown individuals may be spotted with reddish or yellowish dots, as well as irregular blackish blotches, and show a pattern of broad bands on the back and tail; but once the chuckwalla gets to be nine or ten inches long it develops a uniform dull brown color above and sandy

Figure 48. Chuckwalla.

red below, the latter surface spotted with black. The tail is likely to show obscure bands, even in the adult.

As might be judged by the creature's build, this is a rather sluggish, slow-moving reptile. At its best gait it gets over the ground at hardly more than a rapid waddle, although young specimens are agile enough and none-too-easy to catch. The lizard prefers rocky situations, where it can find an abundance of cracks and crevices in which to hide, and it is never very far from some safe haven. If disturbed the chuckwalla squeezes itself into some tight crevice and then inflates its body with air, so that it is all but impossible to pull him out. The animal rarely bites, but if cornered it will defend itself by lashing its rugged tail violently from side to side.

This is one of the few lizards, perhaps the only one, that is commonly used as food in this country. The Indians of the Southwest consider it a great delicacy.

NORTHERN EARLESS LIZARD

Holbrookia maculata Girard

This is a rather chunky little lizard with a tail that is not very long, especially when you compare it with one of the whip-tailed lizards or racerunners. The length of the whole animal, tail included, is about four and one-half inches. Its range is over most of Kansas and Nebraska, excepting only the extreme eastern sections, and it extends into Wyoming, Colorado, Oklahoma, northeastern New Mexico, and the panhandle of Texas. Besides its relatively short tail, this fellow is noted for its long fingers and toes and the fact that it has no external ear-openings.

The chief ground color is dull gray or grayish brown, sometimes tinged with buffy-red at the sides. There is a fairly wide ribbon of pale gray, unspotted, extending down the back and on the tail, with a narrower line paralleling it on each side. Between these longitudinal streaks are a number of dark V-shaped patches, along with several small

Figure 49.   Northern earless lizard.

whitish spots. The V-shaped marks continue part way down the sturdy tail, each dark patch edged at the back with pale gray. On the sides, just below the forelegs, are two diagonal black lines or bars, especially prominent in the males. The underside is plain gray and unspotted, with the throat usually darker in tone. The lower side of the tail is not barred.

The earless lizard, correctly known as the northern or lesser earless lizard to distinguish it from the larger species found in Texas that is called the greater earless lizard, is a creature of sandy wastelands. Its favorite haunts are in dry, open country where vegetation is scrubby and scarce, and even grass is sparse. It is perhaps most abundant on the chalk beds of western Kansas. Strictly diurnal in habits, the lizard is quite active during the daylight hours and may be seen scampering across open spaces, stopping to rest in the shade of some pebble or at the base of some shrub. It is not particularly wary as lizards go but is none too easy to catch without a net of some sort. The earless lizard is well known for its curiosity, and if you are eating your lunch out on the prairie some noon it is more than likely that an individual will take up a position nearby on a clod of earth and watch you intently throughout the performance, almost as if it hoped for a handout. It will do no good to toss it a crumb, however, for it eats nothing but insects, with grasshoppers and spiders high on the list.

The earless lizard does well in captivity. It requires a warm and dry cage, with at least some sunshine during the day. After dark it commonly wriggles itself down into the sand until it is partially buried. For food it will take mealworms, flies, small beetles, crickets, grubs, and similar game. It reproduces by laying eggs, from five to nine, generally in the late summer.

TEXAS EARLESS LIZARD

Holbrookia texana (Troschel)

This is the largest of the earless lizards in this country, a really big individual measuring about six and one-half inches long, of which the tail is more than half. It occurs through-

Figure 50.   Texas earless lizard.

out central and western Texas, across New Mexico, and to central Arizona. It ranges across the border well down into Mexico.

It is an alert and lively little fellow, the body and tail somewhat flattened but rugged and strong, the limbs well developed, and the toes long and slender. The predominant color is gray, or sandy gray, a shade that renders the lizard most inconspicuous in its desert surroundings. There is a series of paired dark spots extending the length of the back, becoming rather broad bars on the dorsal surface of the tail. Along the sides are numerous small round dots of white. Just in front of the junction of the hind legs, and on both sides, are two distinct black bars, generally enclosing a paler area that may be yellowish or even pale orange. These bars extend well around on the underside of the animal. Underneath, the chin and throat are gray with whitish dots, with the rest of the lizard yellowish white. In males there is a bright blue patch at the sides. The lower surface of the tail is white with about a half-dozen bold black bars.

This lizard is at home in rocky situations, in the flatlands bordering deserts, and in the adjoining foothills. It seems to prefer stony surfaces and will scamper quickly across a sandy area and then pause on some boulder or jutting rock. It likes to climb up to the top of such a rock and sit there sunning itself and surveying the surrounding countryside. It is strictly diurnal in habits, living upon ants, beetles, and whatever small insects are in season. When alarmed it dashes away with considerable speed and repeatedly curls its tail up over its back, exposing the boldly marked underside. The flashing black and white pattern evidently confuses a pursuer. It is a fact that when you watch one of these lizards performing, you can see it clearly until it suddenly stops and drops its tail; and then it seems to melt right into the ground and disappear!

Early in the summer about ten eggs are laid, brittle-shelled and white in color. They are buried in dry gravelly soil, sometimes as deep as six inches. They hatch in the late summer.

KEELED EARLESS LIZARD

Holbrookia propinqua Baird and Girard

This lizard is not quite as large as *texana,* averaging about four and one-half inches in length. It is confined to the southeastern part of Texas, ranging south a short distance into Mexico. The scales on its back are small but strongly keeled, a point of difference between this and any other earless lizard of the Southwest.

The over-all color above is brownish gray, with a weak, rather faded pattern of darker marks on the back. The sides bear numerous pale yellow dots. The underside is whitish, dull gray on the throat, and there are two dark bars near the groin. There are no blue patches on the lower sides, marks that are so characteristic in males of the Texas earless lizard, and this species lacks the vivid black and white pattern on the bottom of its tail.

This species is fairly abundant in many localities, preferring sandy wastelands where there is scant vegetation. It is a sun-loving reptile, active during the hottest part of the day and burying itself in loose sand at night.

ZEBRA-TAILED LIZARD

Callisaurus draconoides gabbi Cope

The zebra-tailed lizard, also known as the gridiron-tailed lizard, is a lively little fellow about six inches long, found in our Southwestern states. The typical form, *draconoides* Blainville, occurs in Mexico, in Baja California, and north of the border we have three very closely allied subspecies. The commonest and best known is *gabbi* Cope, which occurs in southern Nevada and central and southern California. It spreads into western Arizona and on down into Mexico. The subspecies *ventralis* (Hallowell) occupies a range in central and southern Arizona; and the subspecies *myurus* Richardson lives in western Nevada, well north of the sections occupied by *gabbi.*

This is a rather slim but well-built lizard. The head is small, blunt, and somewhat flattened, as is the body; but the limbs are long and powerful, with long and slender digits, so that the reptile can get over the ground with astonishing speed. Like several of the desert lizards, it runs on its hind legs when really in a hurry. The scales are smooth and very small. Note that this lizard has an external ear-opening, for otherwise it could easily be mistaken for a slender example of the Texas earless lizard, *Holbrookia texana*, which it resembles very closely.

The color is greenish to dusky gray, thickly speckled with white or pale yellow. The head is generally yellowish gray. Two rows of V-shaped dark blotches extend down the back from the neck to the base of the tail, but these may be indistinct in some specimens. The limbs are dimly cross-banded, and the tail bears strong black bands. There are two distinct diagonal black bars at the sides, just in back of the front legs. The underparts are white, with the bottom of the tail strongly banded with black. The males have a pale blue patch at each side, but during the mating season it becomes bright metallic blue. The throat turns pinkish or orange at this time and is frequently inflated during courtship.

This species has one very unlizard-like habit. When running away from a pursuer, it very commonly curls its tail up over its back after the manner of an Eskimo dog. This reveals the striking black and white pattern and serves to confuse the enemy, although one's first reaction is that it would seem to mark an otherwise harmonizing animal as it scurries across the desert floor. In some cases the lizard runs with its tail held aloft, but more commonly it dashes away for a few yards in a normal position and then stops quickly and raises its tail and waves it slowly from side to side. Then it dashes off again with its tail down. The observer is left staring at the vividly marked flaglike tail, and when this suddenly disappears the eye is not quick enough to adjust to following the rapid movements of the departing lizard. No doubt this is quite effective in thwarting their many attack-

Figure 51.   Zebra-tailed lizard.

ers; and it is interesting to note that the Texas earless lizard, *Holbrookia texana* (Troschel), with a tail pattern nearly the same, has developed exactly the same strategy. During the mating season the males often sit atop some boulder with their tails curled over their backs and do a lot of tail waving, bobbing, and weaving, their throats considerably expanded.

The zebra-tailed lizard appears to be somewhat omnivorous in appetite. It lives chiefly upon insects and spiders but is known to eat plant material also, especially blossoms in the spring. It is extremely active in hunting insects, sometimes leaping a full twelve inches to grab some tempting grasshopper.

Little has been published regarding the breeding habits of this lizard. It is known to lay eggs, usually five or six, sometime in the late summer. Specimens containing eggs have been collected as late as August.

COLORADO DESERT FRINGE-TOED LIZARD

Uma notata Baird

One has only to examine one of these lizards to realize that here is a creature meant to live on the sandy desert. One of its popular names is "sand lizard." The wedge-shaped snout, the underslung jaw, the thick protective eyelids, and the fringe of long scales on one edge of its fingers and toes all point to a creature admirably adapted for a life in sandy wastes, both above and below the surface. These lizards can actually melt into loose sand and "swim" along below the surface. There are three subspecies in this country, all with similar habits and all confined to our extreme Southwest. Perhaps the best known, or at least the typical variety, is *Uma notata notata*.

This lizard is found only in extreme southeastern California and extreme southwestern Arizona. Its range also extends a short distance into Mexico. In short, it is at home in that section of our Southwest that is known as the Colorado Desert. It is a fairly large lizard, attaining an over-all length of close to ten inches. The head is rather short and blunt but with the snout pointed, the limbs are robust and long, the toes quite slender, and the tail is long and gradually tapering. The upper surface is covered with small scales that are smooth. There are external ear openings, protected to some extent by enlarged scales; and a circle of stiff scales surrounds each eye. Most noticeable is a fringe of scales along the outer edge of its toes, particularly the fourth toe of each hind foot.

The pattern on this reptile's back has been compared with that of a jaguar. It is certainly one of our handsomest lizards. The ground color is black; and from the head to the tip of its tail the upper surface is covered with round spots of yellowish gray, most of them with a black center. These spots, which might be called rosettes or ocelli, are often dispersed in longitudinal lines, especially toward the sides. The limbs are gray with solid black dots, and the top of the head is also dotted. The sides may show a buffy tinge, and the underparts are white. There is a distinct black patch on the sides of the belly, the throat and chin bear a few narrow black lines, and there are several jet-black bars on the lower surface of the tail.

This lizard is to be found in the most desolate of sand dunes, where one would scarcely expect any creature to be able to obtain a living. It is probably the only reptile that really shows a preference for such barren wastes. They also occur on low scrubby sand flats but are not likely to be seen in ordinary desert country or in canyons. Their habits are diurnal, and their food consists of ants, beetles, flies, spiders, and similar prey.

In spite of their fringed toes, an obvious adaptation for traveling in loose sand, they are not as fast as some of the whip-tailed lizards or racerunners. They are very speedy, however, and extremely hard to capture uninjured. They are said to "swim" beneath the sand, but what they do is more aptly described as burrowing rapidly beneath the surface. The act is performed when the lizard wishes to escape from the blistering noonday sun and also when alarmed and wanting to hide from some enemy. If there is a rodent burrow handy in either case, it will generally duck into that instead. Stebbins describes the action as follows. "Most fossorial activity appears to be limited to movements not over several times the total length of the animal. Sand-swimming is accomplished by lateral movements of the head and fore parts, accompanied by propulsive movements of the hind feet. The forelimbs are not employed in submergence but lie appressed to the sides. The action of the hind feet and fringes is valvular."

The Coachella Valley fringe-toed Lizard, *Uma notata inornata* Cope, is a very similar subspecies occurring in the Coachella Valley of Riverside County in southern California. There is likely to be less buffy brown along the sides, and this form lacks the conspicuous black marks on the sides of its belly.

Figure 52. Fringe-toed lizard.

COLLARED LIZARD

Crotaphytus collaris (Say)

Many would consider this our most colorful lizard. Possibly this distinction might go to the Gila Monster of our southwestern states or to some other gaily-hued lizard of that area, but there is no overlooking the fact that the collared lizard is very brightly colored indeed. It is a widespread and not uncommon reptile, occurring from Kansas and Missouri south to central Texas and west as far as eastern New Mexico. A very similar subspecies, *Crotaphytus collaris baileyi* (Stejneger), ranges from New Mexico and Arizona to southern California and north to Nevada and Idaho.

The body is plump, and is three or four inches long. The tail is much longer than the body, so the whole animal may be from eight to twelve inches in length. The head is large, quite distinct from the neck, and characteristically held higher than the body. The limbs, especially the hind pair, are long and sturdy.

The upper surface is usually some shade of green, sometimes dull grayish green and sometimes brilliant emerald green, and various shades between. The males are brighter colored and are especially gaudy during the mating season when their throats are bright orange. There are about a half-dozen pale yellow cross-bands on the back, the legs and tail are indistinctly barred, and the whole upper surface bears numerous tiny yellowish dots. At the neck are two black marks, separated by a whitish area. This double "collar" does not ordinarily form a circle, as it fails to cross the throat and is often broken at the back of the neck. The underside is white or bluish white.

The collared lizard is at home in hilly, dry, rocky situations and is an alert, active animal, hopping froglike from rock to rock and running rapidly over the ground. When hard pressed it can travel with uncanny speed, rising upright and dashing along on its hind legs, the long tail held out stiff and acting as a balance. Even when walking leisurely, it commonly holds its tail clear of the ground. The lizard is active all day long, but in very hot and dry sections it is usually quiet during the midday.

This species is a somewhat omnivorous feeder, subsisting chiefly upon insects of various kinds; but it is reported to eat some plant life on occasion and gladly devours any small

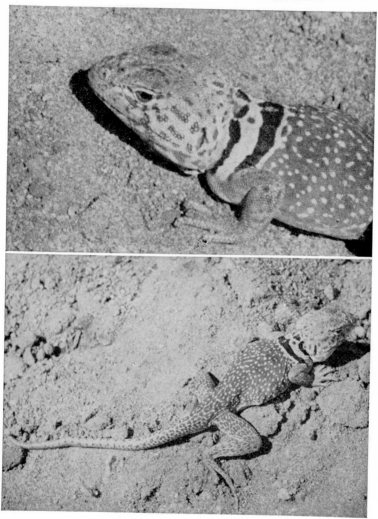

Figure 53. Collared lizard.

lizard or snake it can overpower. It is a pugnacious lizard and will sometimes attack a creature that it could not possibly eat. One writer describes an encounter between a collared lizard and a small rattlesnake. When discovered, the lizard was clinging desperately to the back of the snake's neck and, twist and thrash about as it would, the serpent could not shake the lizard loose. It was evident that the rattler was being slowly choked to death until the watcher took a hand. While the two battlers were being separated, the snake succeeded in striking the lizard on the lower jaw and it died in less than five minutes. If they had been left to themselves, however, the lizard might well have been victorious.

When cornered, this spunky lizard will face its tormentor with widely open mouth, and it does not hesitate to bite, but even the largest individuals cannot exert enough pressure to cause any discomfort. Should a lizard grasp a piece of very loose skin its tiny teeth might possibly pinch a little and even pierce the skin. Some tribes of Southwest Indians call it the "Poisonous Green Lizard" and believe it to be extremely deadly, but of course the collared lizard is quite harmless.

The soft-shelled eggs are deposited four or five inches deep in loose sand. They are oval in shape and about one-half inch long and may number from four or five to about twenty. Captive specimens have laid eggs in August, but in the wild it is probable that this lizard deposits her eggs any time in the late summer.

The collared lizard is a great favorite with travelers in the West. Its quick movements, alert-looking eyes, striking colors, together with its relative abundance make it a popular object with those who are not imbued with the false notion that it is poisonous. It makes a good species for your home terrarium for, although it is not likely ever to show any real affection toward its keeper, it does very well as a rule in confinement and can be taught to take food from your fingers. It must not be kept in an enclosure with smaller lizards, however, for it will attack and kill them. It feeds readily upon mealworms, flies, crickets, grasshoppers, and spiders and will sometimes take small bits of meat dangled before its eyes. It customarily seizes its prey and shakes it, as a bulldog would a rat, before swallowing it.

LEOPARD LIZARD

Crotaphytus wislizeni (Baird and Girard)

The leopard lizard is closely related to the collared lizard just described. It is about the same size, eight to twelve inches long, and has the same general build. It is big headed and long tailed and is very wide-awake and active. Some authorities have placed it in a different genus, *Gambelia*, but most herpetologists today regard it as belonging to the same genus as the collared lizard. It is a creature of desert basins and is found from central Idaho and eastern Oregon southward in suitable locations to western Texas and the eastern desert regions of California.

Figure 54. Leopard lizard.

The color is pale gray or brown above, with several narrow transverse bands of a lighter shade. These bands meet at a mid-dorsal stripe; but very often they are staggered, so that the bands on one side alternate with those on the other. Between the bands are scattered spots that are round in outline and dark in hue. Sometimes the spots are rather large and few in number, but usually they are small and numerous. Along the sides there may be spots of dull red. The tail is boldly spotted and there is no collar. The underside is creamy white, with several longitudinal brown lines on the throat. The females develop a deep salmon color on their undersides at the time of egg laying.

As the animal grows older the transverse lines have a tendency to fade; and many large specimens lack them completely, the back showing only rounded spots of varying sizes. As with many of our lizards, the leopard can alter its color to some degree; and the same individual may be so dark one minute that its spots are scarcely discernible, while in a very short time it may become so pale in shade that its spots are sharply delineated. In this pale phase the reptile's popular name of leopard lizard is most appropriate.

This is an aggressive reptile, overpowering and devouring other lizards nearly as large as itself. It also eats small snakes and an extensive list of insects. Klauber, in his excellent two-volume work on rattlesnakes, reports the following incident from Ira La Rivers, University of Nevada. A large female leopard lizard was placed in a roomy cage with some other lizards and a few snakes, in the summer of 1934. In the morning a small rattlesnake was found stretched out on the floor of the cage, moving feebly, with the leopard lizard firmly attached just behind its head. While Mr. La Rivers watched, the lizard maintained her hold for twenty minutes, during which time the rattler apparently died of suffocation. The lizard was eleven inches long and the rattlesnake was twenty inches long. Of course the lizard could never eat such a victim, and in a wild state such encounters must be very rare, but it illustrates the aggressiveness and courage of this species of lizard.

Unlike the collared lizard, this species is not commonly observed and is seldom encountered in canyons and rocky places. Its preferred home is in the hottest and driest parts of sandy wastes, and in such territory it is not uncommon. One reason it is not as well known as the collared lizard is that the latter species commonly frequents our scenic canyons and National Parks, where it is annually observed by thousands of vacationers, whereas one needs to travel in very inhospitable country to be reasonably sure of seeing the leopard lizard.

THE SPINY LIZARDS

These lizards, all belonging to the genus *Sceloporus*, are known by various names, such as spiny lizards, scaly lizards, sharp-scaled lizards, and scaly swifts, all denoting the sharpness of their dorsal scales and their general bristly appearance. It comprises the largest single group in this country, nearly thirty species and subspecies being recognized. As mentioned earlier, the genus *Anolis* contains many more; but only a couple of them occur in our country, so *Sceloporus* rates first place with us when it comes to numbers of kinds. If we were to include Mexico and Central America, more than one hundred forms are known.

There is considerable variation as to habits and habitat within the group, some preferring brushy hillsides and others sandy flats; some are expert climbers while others appear to prefer staying on the ground. All of them are active daylight lovers; and all are sturdy lizards built on the same general plan, with strong limbs and rugged heads. They are chiefly insectivorous, and some lay eggs while some give birth to living young.

FENCE LIZARD

Sceloporus undulatus (Latreille)

The fence lizard, or common swift, is a fairly abundant reptile over much of this country, being found, in one of its numerous subspecies, from New York to Florida and west as far as the Rocky Mountains. It is absent from the northern tier of states; and its place on the West Coast is taken by a closely related species, *Sceloporus occidentalis* Baird and Girard. The typical *undulatus* is found from the southern part of South Carolina west to Louisiana and south to the central part of Florida.

This lizard is four or five inches long (including the tail), with moderately large, keeled scales that give it a bristly appearance. The tail is rather large, tapering somewhat abruptly; and the limbs are quite sturdy, with toes that are long and provided with sharp claws. The general color is brownish or greenish gray, with a series of narrow, wavy cross-bands of black on the back. In males the undersurface is dark gray or nearly black, with a longitudinal patch of bright blue on each side of the belly. Another pair of blue spots, called gular spots, is present on the throat. The female has a ventral surface that is gray flecked with white, with the paired spots of blue at the throat; but it lacks the blue side patches.

The fence lizard prefers relatively dry situations and is to be looked for in open woods, on sunny wooded hillsides, and in almost any wooded area that is not marshy. It is perhaps most abundant in the dry and sandy pinelands of the Southeast, and probably the best place of all to find specimens is in an area where lumbering operations have recently ceased. On the piles of logs and slabs, and sawdust heaps, the lizard finds good hunting and an abundance of crevices and holes in which to hide. It normally lives on the ground, among the rocks and fallen trees, about stone walls and rail fences, and frequently about buildings that have been abandoned. It is a good climber, although it does not ascend trees to any great height. A pursued specimen will often run up a tree trunk and circle the tree like a squirrel, keeping out of sight in an expert manner.

The fence lizard is a shy creature, agile and swift in its movements, and not very easy to capture without a noose. The tail is rather easily detached; and some individuals, even when pinned down by the shoulders, twist and squirm until it becomes separated from the body. It requires several weeks to grow a new tail, so it is not at all uncommon to see fence lizards with tails in all stages of regeneration.

In the spring, when temperatures are warm, the fence lizard lays its eggs, which may number from three or four to a dozen or more. They are about three-fourths of an inch long and white in color. By hatching time, they are some-

Figure 55. Northern fence lizard. The specimen shown in the upper picture has a regenerated tail. Compare its length with the tail of the specimen in the lower picture.

what larger and are dull gray in hue. They are deposited
in a burrow that the lizard digs and afterwards covers up, so
that they rest two or three inches beneath the surface. Dry,
sandy soil is preferred. Hatching takes place in from eight
to twelve weeks. The young lizards grow quite rapidly and
are fully mature by the following spring.

The northern subspecies, *Sceloporus undulatus hyacinthinus* (Green), enjoys a much wider distribution than the
typical *undulatus*. It has not been recorded from any of the
New England states but has been taken in New York, and
west through Pennsylvania and southern Ohio and Indiana
to Oklahoma, and south to the Gulf in eastern Texas. In
more Eastern states, its southern range extends to central
Georgia and Alabama, there meeting the northern limits of
the typical *undulatus*.

The northern fence lizard is usually a little less sharply
marked than its southern relative and commonly averages a
bit smaller in size. It has a greater number of dorsal scales,
a fact which aids the specialist in areas on the borderline
where the two subspecies meet; but generally speaking it is
the only rough, spiny-scaled lizard to be seen throughout
most of its range, so its identification is seldom in doubt.

The habits of this subspecies are essentially the same as
those of the one just discussed. It is active during the daylight hours, spending the nights sleeping under loose bark
or in some crevice where it can find concealment. Its breeding season is later in the year as one goes north and may be
as late as the first part of July in some localities.

NORTHWESTERN FENCE LIZARD

Sceloporus occidentalis Baird and Girard

This is the common scaly lizard of the West Coast, sometimes called the Pacific fence lizard. It occurs from the
middle sections of California all the way up to British Columbia, ranging inland throughout most of California and to
about the central parts of Oregon and Washington. East-

Figure 56.   Northwestern fence lizard.

ward, throughout Nevada and well into Utah, we find the subspecies *biseriatus* Hallowell.

The northwestern fence lizard is nearly five inches long from snout to tail-tip and is a ruggedly built animal, very quick in its movements. The color above is gray or brown, generally with a double row of triangular dark spots on the back, the spots edged behind with green. The sides are buffy, more or less mottled with darker hues; and the lower surface is gray, commonly with a pair of black median lines. There are a pair of bright blue patches on the sides of the belly, usually bordered by black.

Like the fence lizard of the East, this one seeks a home where it can find an abundance of places in which to take refuge when danger threatens. It is found about old fences and walls, abandoned buildings, in brushy tangles of slide rock, and on weedy hillsides where there are numerous burrows of ground squirrels and gophers. It is diurnal in habit and is prone to sun itself at midday on some projecting tree root or stone. It is an expert climber and can run up a tree with the agility of a squirrel but spends by far the greater portion of its life on the ground.

Sceloporus occidentalis biseriatus Hallowell is popularly known as the San Joaquin fence lizard. This is a subspecies whose range includes most of Nevada, western Utah, and north into Idaho and eastern Oregon and Washington. In the south it extends into California, replacing the typical *occidentalis* in the southern part of that state, and on down into Baja California.

This is a slightly larger lizard than the typical *occidentalis*. The color above is gray or olive brown, generally with a rather wide dark stripe at the sides; and there is a series of dark brown or black undulating marks on the back. The customary blue patches are present on the lower sides. This is the common scaly lizard in southern California, at home almost everywhere it can find rocky or stony territory. It, too, is an adept climber and can scamper up the perpendicular side of a rock with astonishing ease. Its general habits are much the same as those of its close relative, *occidentalis*.

FLORIDA SCRUB LIZARD

Sceloporus woodi Stejneger

This lizard lives in the peninsular part of Florida, occurring wherever it can find suitable ecologic conditions. It is not a very big member of the scaly lizard group, seldom exceeding five inches in over-all length. Like the others, it has large keeled scales on its back, strong and sturdy limbs, and an alert, wide-awake look that seems to be characteristic of the genus *Sceloporus*.

The color above is brown, or gray-brown, with a prominent dark lateral stripe that begins on the side of the neck and extends to the base of the tail. Between these two dark stripes the animal may be plain gray, but more often there is a series of paired dark patches that continue part way down on the tail. The underside is white or creamy white, the throat sometimes spotted with black and bearing a pair of black-bordered blue patches. The sides of the belly also

Figure 57. Florida scrub lizard.

show blue areas; those, too, often bordered with black. The females are marked like the males, with the ventral blue areas weaker and generally smaller.

In Florida this reptile is commonly known as the scrub pine lizard. It inhabits the scrub pine country, which is a dry and sandy territory in central and southeastern Florida with a preponderance of pines, dwarf palmettos, rosemary bushes, and various small, scrubby vines and shrubs. The lizard is a very good climber, but is said commonly to seek escape by running across the sand like a racerunner or whip-tailed lizard rather than to hide in crevices or dodge around the trunk of a tree to avoid capture.

SAGEBRUSH LIZARD

Sceloporus graciosus Baird and Girard

This is a fairly common ground lizard, or ground swift, in our western mountain states, ranging from Montana south to northern Arizona and New Mexico and from Colorado to eastern California. In the Far West its place is taken by a subspecies, *Sceloporus graciosus gracilis* Baird and Girard, this latter form occupying much of California, Oregon, and Washington.

The sagebrush lizard is not very big. Its length, including the long tail, is about five or six inches. Like the other swifts, this is a scaly fellow, its back being covered with sharp scales that are strongly keeled. The general color is greenish gray, with a longitudinal stripe along each side that upon close examination proves to be made up of a series of closely packed brown spots. A similar stripe runs from the eye to the base of the tail, the two separated by a paler band. The underside is grayish white, in the case of the females almost completely so; but with males the throat is sometimes mottled with blue, and the belly shows intensely blue patches on either side.

As might be inferred from its popular name, this lizard is most at home in sagebrush country. It lives on the slopes of mountains as well as on desert floors and rarely does any climbing, seeming content to stay on the ground most of the time. When alarmed it takes refuge under a stone or in some crevice among the rocks or scampers into some mammal burrow. Like the other swifts, it is strictly diurnal in habits. Insects make up almost all of its food, and possibly the species is completely insectivorous. All kinds of insects are eaten, the reptile showing little preference and generally feeding upon the kinds that are most abundant and easily captured at various seasons of the year. Ants are probably the chief standby during the entire warm season that the sagebrush lizard is active.

Like all of the swifts, this one lives up to its name, and is not very easy to catch. It does well in captivity if it can be supplied with a steady stock of live insects. It will accept mealworms and flies, grasshoppers if not too large, and crickets, spiders, and cockroaches. It shows no interest whatever in earthworms. From four to seven eggs are laid in early summer, generally the first part of July, and are buried an inch or so deep in loose sand. They hatch in about six weeks.

The subspecies *gracilis* differs from the typical *graciosus* in having smaller scales on its back, in having a blue throat (males only), and in averaging a bit smaller in size.

TEXAS SPINY LIZARD

Sceloporus olivaceus Smith

This species is at home over most of central Texas, as its common name implies. It ranges well down into Mexico, while to the north it just does get into the southern part of Oklahoma. It appears to be absent from the eastern parts of Texas, as well as the western sections. It is a spiny reptile, attaining a total length of about eight inches, with the average specimen measuring between five and six.

The color is dull grayish brown, with an irregular paler stripe down each side of the back. Several wavy crossbars are present on the upper surface; and the sides are darker in tone, flecked with paler spots. The underside is grayish white, sometimes with a dark median line that is made up of broken dots. The sides of the belly are decorated with rather small light blue areas in the case of males, but these are lacking in females.

This is a climbing, or tree lizard, and is to be looked for in wooded areas. It is generally fairly abundant on any kind of tree; but its favorites seem to be hackberry, mesquite, and live oak. Its chief concern is to have a tree that will provide safe places of refuge in the shape of knotholes or crevices—any snug retreat in which they can hide from their enemies. They depend upon their highly successful protective coloration to a large extent, and when motionless against the bark they are indeed astonishingly hard to see. They are equally at home about old barns and abandoned outbuildings, climbing about over the rough boards with the utmost ease.

DESERT SPINY LIZARD

Sceloporus magister Hallowell

The desert spiny lizard is at home in the arid Southwest, the center of abundance being Arizona. It ranges eastward well into New Mexico and western Texas and westward to California; to the north, it occurs in Nevada and Utah and to the south its range extends well into Mexico. It is a large and rugged lizard, measuring about twelve inches from snout to tail-tip when fully grown.

This swift is dressed in large and sharp scales on its back, has a long and heavily scaled tail, and robust limbs with long and sharp digits. The head is relatively massive but surprisingly short. The over-all color is brown on the upper surface and grayish white below, the sides somewhat darker in tone. Indistinct transverse bars are present on the back, and the limbs and tail may be weakly banded. There is usually a pronounced dark patch just in front of each fore-leg, these patches extending up and part way across the back to suggest a sort of collar. The male has a light blue throat, and his underside is deep blue at the sides. The female has a grayish white belly, with no blue in evidence.

This lizard is a good climber and is at home where there is ample cover, such as rock piles and tangled thickets. It is likely to spend most of its time on the ground but can scurry up a pine or cottonwood tree or even a telephone pole almost as quickly as a squirrel. It much prefers to seek refuge in a ground hole if possible but in an emergency will flatten out on a branch or in a crotch and remain motionless until the danger has passed. They are usually absent in areas where there is scanty vegetation and should not be looked for in open desert country. They are very quick in their movements, alert and cautious, and generally very difficult to capture alive and unhurt.

The desert spiny lizard is chiefly an insect eater, consuming vast quantities of ants, flies, beetles, and grasshoppers. They do not hesitate to devour any small lizards they

Figure 58.   Desert spiny lizard (and eggs).

can catch and are known to eat plants to some extent. In captivity they will accept mealworms and spiders, rushing upon their prey in a most ferocious manner. If you keep lizards in a terrarium, do not put this species in with any others, particularly if they are smaller in size. The desert spiny lizard is an aggressive and pugnacious reptile and is quarrelsome to boot. The author once placed a fine female specimen in the same cage with several other lizards, all at

least as large as *magister*. The next morning, a splendid
whip-tailed lizard was dead, its head chewed almost off,
although in total length the whip-tail had outstretched the
spiny lizard by nearly two inches.

CLARK'S SPINY LIZARD

Sceloporus clarki Baird and Girard

This species is more widespread in Mexico than it is in
this country but is fairly common in southwestern New
Mexico and southeastern Arizona. It gets to be some nine
or ten inches long from its nose to its tail-tip, the tail measuring more than half of this length.

Clark's spiny lizard is a rugged and spiny fellow, with
dorsal scales that are large, sharp, and strongly keeled. The
limbs are sturdy, with long fingers and toes; the head is
relatively large; and, as indicated above, the tail is well developed. The color above is gray, verging on pale blue,
with indistinct crossbars on the back. A distinct dark band
is generally present on the shoulders. The limbs and tail

Figure 59.   Clark's spiny lizard.

also show crossbars, usually stronger than those on the back. Underneath, the males have a blue throat and bluish or greenish patches on the sides of the belly. These areas are mottled gray and black in the females.

This is essentially a climbing species, being most at home on wooded plateaus where it scampers about over fallen timbers and ascends well up in the trees. In regions that are treeless it gets along very well by doing its climbing on boulders and rocky surfaces in general. It is rarely seen on the ground, and sections that are without both trees and boulders are usually without Clark's lizards too.

Like many of the arboreal lizards, this one will scurry around a tree when pursued, keeping the trunk or branch between itself and its pursuer. When hard-pressed it will take refuge in cracks and crevices or beneath boulders and in rock fissures. It is not, however, as wary as many of the ground dwellers and is usually not very hard to capture. It does well in captivity, accepting mealworms with evident satisfaction. In its native state it lives chiefly upon insects, with ants and beetles high on the list. It lays a dozen or more eggs in the spring, which are buried in a shallow excavation in loose soil.

YARROW'S SPINY LIZARD

Sceloporus jarrovi Cope

This is one of the most striking in appearance of any of our lizards, but it very nearly misses our country altogether. It is found in much of Mexico and does range up as far as southeastern Arizona and southwestern New Mexico. It is a solidly built reptile, averaging about seven inches in length when adult.

The color is black above, with a yellowish, almost golden, spot in the center of each scale. The animal's back glistens like burnished copper when the light strikes it from certain angles. There is a prominent dark collar that doesn't quite meet over the shoulders; and the head is mostly black, with

Figure 60. Yarrow's spiny lizard.

paler shades around the mouth and a pale line running back
from each eye. The robust tail is very scaly and is marked
like the lizard's back, with just a suggestion of banding, but
it becomes black at its end. The underside is largely blue,
the throat and sides brilliantly hued, and the belly paler in
tone. Females lack these bright colors, being speckled gray
and white above and grayish below, sometimes showing a
yellowish cast to their dorsal scales. They do have the distinguishing black collar.

Yarrow's spiny lizard is certainly one of the most colorful and attractive of our lizards; and it is also one of our
boldest, so it is not at all hard to observe if one visits its
natural haunts. It is essentially a reptile of high country
and prefers mountain regions at an elevation of seven or
eight thousand feet. Here it is at home in a variety of situations and appears to be completely happy in sun-drenched
canyons, about trees and prostrate logs and abandoned
cabins, along mountain streams, and even in heavily forested

areas of oak or pine, provided there are boulders and fallen logs scattered about on the ground.

Probably few lizards enjoy sun bathing any more than this one. On bright days they may be seen resting on boulders, dead branches and bark, or on exposed ledges of rock, anywhere they can soak up the warm sunshine. They are ordinarily quite without fear at such times, and one can usually advance to within a few feet without frightening them away. A favorite method of capturing them is to make a noose of black thread and fasten it to the end of a slender stick. Yarrow's lizard will generally stand rigidly while you reach out and slip the noose over its head. Should you miss on your first attempt, the lizard will commonly stay right where it is while you try again, sometimes even chewing on the thread, but still without any ideas about escaping. Indian children make nooses of grass for this sport. Large adults are generally more wary than partly grown individuals; but all in all this is a rather fearless lizard, and a welcome change from the many kinds that scurry for safety long before you are within "noosing" range.

This is another of the relatively few American lizards that give birth to living young instead of laying eggs. The young are usually few in number, often only two or three, and are born in the summer. It would seem that these live-bearing lizards would enjoy a marked advantage over the egg layers, for many lizards and snakes, as well as birds and mammals, are ever ready to make a meal of a nest of eggs whenever they can find one; but the fact that the baby lizards come into the world ready, within hours, to run rapidly and hide, should be important in the survival of the race.

CREVICE SPINY LIZARD

Sceloporus poinsetti Baird and Girard

This is another large scaly lizard. It is robust in build, with a rather blunt head. The color above is gray, shading to rusty red on the sides, with four or five dark transverse bars on the back; just back of the head is a bar that is generally black and sharply delineated, forming a distinct collar. The tail is strongly banded; but the limbs are usually plain gray, more or less mottled. Males have a bright blue throat and blue borders on their white bellies, while females show a white underside, sometimes with gray at the throat and sides. Due to the quite noticeable rust-colored sides of this particular species, it is sometimes known as the red scaly lizard.

This is also a lover of hot, dry country, being found in southern New Mexico and southwestern Texas and ranging well down into Old Mexico. It is a creature of boulder-strewn wastelands, rocky canyons, and limestone cliffs. It gets its popular name from the fact that it habitually takes refuge in the crevices and fissures of its stony environment. An excellent climber on rocky surfaces, it seldom climbs the thorny bushes or shrubs that may dot the landscape but prefers to scamper from rock to rock or from boulder to boulder. It is one of the hardest of all lizards to take alive and unhurt, for once it gets firmly wedged in a crack or crevice it usually cannot be withdrawn without damage to a limb or tail.

The crevice spiny lizard is an insect eater, subsisting on ants, flies, beetles, spiders, and similar prey. The young are born alive, in the spring, and number up to ten.

LONG-TAILED BRUSH LIZARD

Uta graciosus Hallowell

The interesting group of small lizards, long known as the genus *Uta*, has been split up into three genera by many modern workers. Those living chiefly on rocks are placed in the genus *Petrosaurus*, those living in trees in the genus *Urosaurus*, and those that live chiefly on the ground are left in the genus *Uta*. For our purpose we shall consider them all under the generic name of *Uta*.

The long-tailed brush lizard is a trim little animal, its over-all length close to seven inches, with the long tail making up nearly two-thirds of its total length. It may be said to live throughout the Colorado Valley, occurring as it does in southeastern California and western Arizona and in southern Nevada. This is a slender species, with a relatively long head and sturdy limbs and long fingers and toes. There are several large plate-like scales on top of the head, and down the center of the back are a couple of rows of scales that are larger than the rest on the dorsal surface. The exceptionally long tail gives this species its popular name.

The general ground color is gray, or sandy gray, above, and grayish white below. The upper surface shows longitudinal lines toward the sides and between them a pattern of irregular and broken transverse bars, all only slightly darker in tone than the ground color. The head bears a pattern of narrow dark lines. The males have blue patches at the groin, and their throats may be darker or more or less streaked; while the lower parts of females are dusky gray, sometimes mottled or speckled on the throat and chest.

They feed upon insects and spiders, and much of their prey can be obtained among the branches; but they descend to the ground and forage around for ants, ground beetles, etc. When danger threatens they are likely to leap into the nearest bush rather than to escape by running over the ground. However, when a person really goes into the bush after them, and they are aware that they are no longer safely concealed, they quickly drop to the ground and take refuge in holes or under stones. Collectors report that the simplest method for obtaining this species is to go out at night and carefully examine each branch with a flashlight. Their pale undersides show up clearly in the rays of the light, and it is often possible to collect several specimens from a single creosote or mesquite bush.

The rapid color changes of these lizards are well known. During the hottest part of the day they may become almost brilliant, the dark markings standing out vividly, and the

yellows and blues showing clearly along the sides. A few
minutes later the same individual becomes dull brown or so
pale a gray that it looks almost white. Little has been written about their breeding habits, other than the fact that they
lay eggs.

TEXAS TREE LIZARD

Uta ornata Baird and Girard

This is a rather small reptile, its length usually no more
than four and one-half inches, of which the tail constitutes
considerably more than half. The typical form is found in
central Texas, and several subspecies extend the lizard's
range as far as California and Utah.

The color is brownish gray, with a series of paired irregular blotches on the back. The front pair, at the shoulders,
is nearly black, giving the animal a sort of collar; and the
rest are paler in tone and are generally edged in back by
white or pale blue. The limbs are barred, even including the

Figure 61.   Texas tree lizard.

toes; and the head, which is lighter in shade than the body, bears thin brown lines, often in the shape of an arrowhead. There is a white streak on the sides of the neck. The underside is gray, with the males sporting blue throats and blue patches at the sides.

This is decidedly an arboreal lizard, almost always found in a tree. Perhaps it may be seen on the sunny side of some old weather-beaten barn or scampering quickly along a rail fence, but it is not often that a specimen is observed on the ground. Probably no lizard is more adept at keeping a tree trunk or a limb between itself and a pursuer. Its habits are strictly diurnal; and it is likely to be most active in the morning and again in the afternoon, with a quiescent period during the middle of the day. It sleeps at night flattened out on a branch or tucked into some crevice in the bark.

SIDE-BLOTCHED LIZARD

Uta stansburiana Baird and Girard

This little lizard is a rather common inhabitant of our western country, from Washington down through Oregon and Idaho, northeastern California, and across Nevada and Utah to western Colorado. It also occurs in the northern sections of Arizona and New Mexico, but a couple of subspecies replace it further south and west. It is a neat little lizard, with a short but broad head, a robust body, and a long tapering tail. The limbs are sturdy, the fingers and toes long and slender. The total length is about four inches.

The over-all color is gray, sometimes quite pale and sometimes rather dark; and the whole upper surface is dotted with small roundish paler spots. The spots at the sides are usually larger than those on the back. Sometimes the dorsal spots may be fused more or less regularly to suggest a weak pattern of blotchy chevrons, but mostly this lizard can best be described by the term "speckled." The sexes are colored alike, and both have grayish underparts.

This is a ground lizard by choice. It is perfectly capable

Figure 62. Side-blotched lizard.

of climbing into the bushes and on bare rocks, but it spends by far the greater part of its time on the ground. One of its popular names is ground lizard or ground uta. Occurring over such a wide territory, it seems to adapt itself to various ecological conditions and may be found in rocky canyons, on high plateaus, and on low desert flats; but its preferred habitat is on loose gravelly soil where there are a few scattered sagebrush or other bushes. It has been noted that those specimens living in rocky places tend to be brownish in tone, those in sandy regions more grayish, and those from brush-covered hillsides may be olive in hue.

The side-blotched lizards are less wary than many others, and as a general rule they are not especially hard to catch. They attempt to escape by running, but they don't go very fast or very far before they nudge up against a rock or squirm under a stone and "freeze," and it is a simple task to grab them. They spend the nights under stones or buried in the sands or gravels around roots and are active all during the day, except the hottest midday period. At this time they rest in the shade of some plant and often may be found congregated under particularly shady examples of cactus or other broadleaf shrubs.

They eat almost any small crawling thing, including spiders, millepedes, and scorpions, and of course greedily devour any sort of insect that is not too large to handle conveniently. In the sugar beet country of Utah these lizards are regarded as extremely beneficial animals, since they annually destroy vast numbers of the beet leafhopper. The species does very well in captivity, getting over their original fright quite soon and becoming tame in a short time. Late in June the female lays four or five oval white eggs and conceals them in loose gravel, just under the surface. They hatch in late August.

BANDED ROCK LIZARD

Uta mearnsi Stejneger

This lizard is at home in the Mexican peninsula of Baja California; but its range extends north into southern California, so it is a good United States species. It is a sizeable reptile, attaining a length of ten or eleven inches, including its long whiplike tail. It is a robust animal, with a large flattened head; in fact, the whole body appears rather flattish.

Its color is gray or olive gray, with a mid-dorsal stripe from which bars of the same shade extend out over the sides. Just back of the neck one of these bars is black, giving the effect of a collar. The tail is banded, and over the whole upper surface the skin is peppered with small dots of bluish white. The underside is nearly all dark blue, almost indigo, in the case of males.

At first glance this lizard resembles the familiar collared lizard (*Crotaphytus collaris*) of our Western states, but a closer examination shows that it is quite different. It is always found in boulder-strewn canyons or similar rocky situations and never on sandy or brushy flats; in fact, it refuses to live anywhere but amid the broken and fissured floors of canyons. Not very much has been written about this species, but it is reported as not overly wary, and when it is alarmed it takes refuge in cracks and crannies between the rocks. Its habits are diurnal, and it is reported most active in the early part of the day and again in the late afternoon.

Its food consists of beetles, spiders, and similar prey; and it is known to eat some plant material, such as tender buds and flowers. It is an egg layer, depositing two to four white eggs in June. Many herpetologists place this lizard in a separate genus and list it as *Streptosaurus mearnsi* (Stejneger).

TEXAS HORNED LIZARD

Phrynosoma cornutum (Harlan)

The "horned toad" is dear to the heart of many travelers in the Southwest, seeming to symbolize the sun-drenched deserts and their spiny inhabitants. Of course it is a perfectly good lizard and not a toad at all; but there is ample reason for its popular name, as the animal is certainly toadlike in its appearance and to some extent in its behavior as well.

There are about a half-dozen species of these interesting little reptiles, as well as several subspecies; but the Texas horned lizard is perhaps the commonest form, enjoying the widest distribution, and is the one usually brought back East in a shoebox. It is found from Kansas south through most of Texas into northern Mexico and west to southern Arizona. Throughout much of this territory it is the only horned lizard found.

The length is about five inches over-all. It has a wide, rounded, much flattened body; a very short tail; and short limbs. The scales on the back are mostly very small, but among them rise others that are very large and sharply pointed. The scales are keeled, even those on the belly, this last feature being a point of difference between this species and the other horned lizards. There is a fringe of sawlike scales along each side and on the front edge of the fore limbs. The head is large but short and is carried erect. Prominent bony ridges over the eyes give the animal an alert, wide-

Figure 63.   *Above:* Texas horned lizard.   *Below:* Close-up of a top view of the head.

awake look. The back of the head is crowned with a row of long, sharp spines (which must make the creature a disagreeable fellow to swallow, from the viewpoint of a snake). An additional nublike horn is present over each eye.

The horned lizard is colored in soft grays and browns, as one would expect in a desert dweller. There is a rather prominent narrow yellowish stripe running from just back of the head to near the end of the tail. A pair of dark, crescent-shaped blotches are present on the neck, one on each side of this median line, while three more pairs are found on the body. The general ground color is dull gray, or sandy gray; and the reptile blends so perfectly with its surroundings that it has no real need for speed, depending instead on camouflage for its protection.

The horned lizard is strictly diurnal in habits and is most active during the late afternoon. It is a ground lover and does no climbing other than scrambling up on stones or rocks. It seeks its food somewhat like a toad. Where the sagebrush swift, for example, might sight an insect a few inches away and capture it with a lightning-like rush, the horned lizard would stalk it deliberately until close enough, then study the situation carefully for a proper length of time before bending its head to the right angle, then thrust out its tongue with incredible speed, and the insect would be his, the whole performance reminding one very strongly of a feeding toad. Ants constitute its chief food, but almost any small insect that chances to get within range is gratefully accepted.

At night, and on cloudy days, the horned lizard scoops out a shallow depression in the sand and with much wriggling and squirming manages to bury itself partially, leaving only the head uncovered. The body is so flattened that one finds it hard to believe that the creature has any insides. During the winter months it hibernates six or seven inches deep in the sand.

Some of our horned lizards give birth to living young, but this species lays eggs. As many as twenty-five are laid in late May or early June and are buried in loose soil or sand to a depth of about five inches. They hatch in early August, and the little fellows are well able to take care of themselves as soon as they have succeeded in clawing their way to the surface.

We hear a good many mythical stories about our reptiles, such as the tale of the "hoop snake." One story attributed to this little lizard, although little short of fantastic, is absolutely true! This concerns the animal's ability to eject a thin stream of blood from the corner of each eye when it is greatly alarmed. Dr. Ditmars reported an individual squirting a threadlike stream a distance of four feet, where it splattered against a wall at the same height as the lizard's eyes. Just what advantage, or survival value, this practice has for the reptile is a little hard to guess. It seems unlikely that an enemy would thus be put to flight, and a momentary confusion would be of no practical help to so slow-moving a creature. It is certain that neither the blood nor anything else about the horned lizard is harmful.

DESERT HORNED LIZARD

Phrynosoma platyrhinos Girard

The desert horned lizard occurs in our Far Western states but not along the Pacific coastal regions. It may be found from extreme southeastern Washington through eastern Oregon and southwestern Idaho, throughout practically all of Nevada, and south through eastern California and western Arizona, down into Mexico.

This is a fair-sized species, some five inches in length, and is round and flattish like the other "horned toads." The general color is pale brown, with a paler narrow median streak down the middle of the back and a series of black, jagged blotches on either side, so that the back is decorated with rather sharply defined markings that are white edged behind. The tail is strongly banded, and the limbs generally show banding or mottling. The underside is soiled white with a few black dots. There are scattered rusty

Figure 64.   Desert horned lizard.

marks on the upper surface, particularly near the head. All
in all, this is a rather colorful member of its group. The
colors vary considerably, and the same individual may be
richly colored with browns and rusty orange at one time
and drab grayish brown a few minutes later. The color
changes are dependent on temperature, bright sunlight,
emotions, or combinations of all three.

The head is crowned with long spines; and there is a
short, nublike spine above and back of each eye. The scales
on the back are numerous and sharp, and there is a fringe of
short spines along the sides and continuing on down the tail
and is even present on the front edge of the forelimbs.

As its popular name implies, this is a creature of sun-
drenched desert country. It is not likely to be found in vast
expanses of sand but requires some cover in the form of
rocks or low desert plants. It is active during the daylight
hours and may be seen contentedly squatting on a rock at
midday in broiling sun that would seem most uncomfortable.
Its food consists chiefly of ants, with an occasional beetle or
other insect. At night it partially buries itself in the sand,

with only its head uncovered. It hibernates deeper in sand
or gravel during the winter months, to reappear sometime
in the spring, when the sands are once more well heated.

This species also makes a fine pet if it is kept in a warm
and dry place, given some sunshine part of the day, and a
plentiful supply of small insects. A few drops of water
sprinkled on the vegetation in its cage every three or four

Figure 65. San Diego horned lizard.

days will take care of its drinking needs. It is a very mild-mannered reptile, never trying to bite and seldom making any attempt to escape. Even wild specimens often submit to capture quite readily.

Next to the Texas horned lizard, *Phrynosoma cornutum*, this is the most widely distributed and abundant of the "horned toads." It is another egg-laying form, about a dozen eggs that are roundish and white being laid in May or June. They are deposited in an excavation five or six inches deep in gravelly sand and hatch in four or five weeks.

Two other horned lizards are found in California. The so-called San Diego horned lizard, *Phrynosoma coronatum blainvillei* Gray, occurs in the southern part of the state and on into Baja California; and the California horned lizard, *Phrynosoma coronatum frontale* Van Denburgh, occurs further north to well above San Francisco and is also found in Baja California. Curiously enough, there is an area between the two colonies where this subspecies does not occur. The typical *coronatum* Blainville is confined to Mexico.

These two lizards are about the same in size, coloration, habits, and general appearance and are distinguished by certain differences in scalation. Both occur further west than the better-known *platyrhinos* just discussed.

SHORT-HORNED LIZARD

Phrynosoma douglasi (Bell)

This is the most northern representative of the "horned toads," being found from southern British Columbia down through eastern Washington and Oregon and in Idaho to northern California. A subspecies occurs from Montana through Wyoming to northeastern Kansas, and other closely related forms are found from Idaho south through the mountain states to Arizona and New Mexico and on down into Old Mexico.

In Mexico there is a similar species named *Phrynosoma orbiculare*, also with several subspecies; and many authorities contend that the two groups should be united as a single complex. If that is done the older name, *orbiculare*, would have to be used; and the horned lizard under discussion would be listed as *Phrynosoma orbiculare douglasi*.

This is a small lizard, seldom exceeding four inches in length, tail and all. It is a stubby little fellow, broad and flat like the others, its dorsal surface well covered with small but sharp scales, some of them enlarged and keeled. The "horns" adorning the head are quite small, much shorter than in the case of the Texas or desert horned lizards.

The general color is gray or brown, sometimes with a yellowish tinge; and the shades are generally dull and faded. There are several dark blotches on the back, the blotches being edged with white behind and blending into the ground color in front. The tail is usually banded, the limbs more or less spotted or marbled, and the underside is whitish or yellowish.

Although this lizard is at home in what we are likely to think of as mountainous country, its preferred territory is in the valleys and open plains where there is an abundance of broken rock and gravelly sand. Like the others, it enjoys basking in the sun, is strictly diurnal in habits, and feeds upon ants and other small insects. Of course, it is entirely harmless.

The short-horned lizard does not lay eggs but gives birth to living young. Actually, the mother carries the eggs until they are ready to hatch; and hatching takes place within her body, so the young are produced alive. They are only about an inch long and may number from six or seven up to as many as thirty.

DESERT NIGHT LIZARD

Xantusia vigilis Baird

The night lizards make up a small group of unusual lizards, some four or five kinds being recognized in this country, all in the Southwest. The genus extends down through Mex-

ico and Central America and is known in Cuba. They have
large eyes with vertical pupils and no eyelids at all. Their
backs are granular and often tuberculated, and their bellies
are covered by broad rectangular plates. As their name implies, they are strictly nocturnal and are not often observed,
although they are not exactly rare. All of them give birth
to living young.

Figure 66.   Desert night lizard.

Perhaps the commonest and best known of the group is the desert night lizard, *Xantusia vigilis*. It occurs in southern Nevada and over much of southern California. Its range includes the southwestern tip of Utah and the northwestern corner of Arizona. It is a small lizard, averaging less than four inches in length, with its tail making up about half. It is a delicate little fellow; its back adorned with tiny scales and tubercles; and its underside showing broad, transverse, platelike scales. There is a deep fold at the throat called a gular fold. The head is rather flat and pointed and is covered on top with large plates. The eyes are lidless and have vertical pupils (round at night), and there are rather large ear openings. The limbs are small, and the tail is long and slender.

The color varies from yellowish gray to brown, with numerous small dark brown or black spots which sometimes run together to suggest elongate bars. The limbs and tail are marked like the back, while the underside is white or grayish white. Some individuals may be very pale, with scarcely any dotting, while others are so heavily dotted that the ground color hardly shows at all.

The desert night lizard is found in desert country, as one would expect, its favorite spot being some semiarid flatland where there is an abundance of debris, such as fallen and decaying branches and trunks of Joshua trees under which it can hide. It lurks under other plants and shrubs and beneath flat stones and boards if any are present. It apparently stays concealed throughout the day. When disturbed, the lizard will not run very far or very fast but will usually climb the first object it comes to; sometimes, as one collector states, it will climb up a collector's trouser leg in a frenzied attempt to escape.

Barring a disturbance of some kind, these lizards are probably never out in the sunshine. The author once had a fine specimen sent by mail from Arizona. Desiring to take a few photographs, I placed the reptile on a patch of sand in a sunny location for that purpose. Now, the sun's rays in Connecticut are not nearly as hot as they are in Arizona; but in less than one minute my lizard showed evident signs of distress; and in three minutes it appeared almost dead. I hastily dug a hole in the sand, in the shade, and down where the earth was damp and cool, dropped the lizard in. It revived in a short time. Again putting the little fellow out in the sun brought the same result—a nearly dead lizard in just a few short minutes. This same individual, revived again, lived for several weeks in a terrarium; but it spent most of the daytime hiding under a piece of bark.

Their food consists of small insects, including ants, termites, flies, and beetles. The young are born alive and generally number but one or two.

In a narrow belt across west central Arizona we find a very similar species, known as the Arizona night lizard, *Xantusia arizonae* Klauber. It is marked very much like the one just described and differs from it chiefly in the matter of scalation. It is not a common form and is not too well known, although it is said to rest under stones and chips of rock more than beneath rotting wood. Presumably its habits are essentially the same as those of the desert night lizard.

GRANITE NIGHT LIZARD

Xantusia henshawi Stejneger

This little lizard occurs in southern California and ranges well down into Baja California. It is not found near the coast but is at home on the slopes of the interior mountain ranges. Its length is about four inches.

It is a trim little reptile, with a rather large head, a long tapering tail, and sturdy limbs. The body is somewhat flattened. The scales on its back are tiny and granular, while those on its belly are large and broad, forming distinct bands across the ventral surface. The ear openings are large and plainly visible, and the eyes are without lids. The pupils are vertical in daylight.

The color is yellowish gray; and the upper surface is ornamented with large, roundish, dark brown spots that are

Figure 67. Granite night lizard.

scattered haphazardly over the back from just behind the eyes all the way to the end of the tail. The legs are more or less marbled, and the whole underside is yellowish white.

This lizard is well named, for it certainly does show a marked preference for granite boulders and will rarely be seen in any other kind of environment. It is a swift-moving little fellow, able to climb about over the rocks with supreme agility; and it is not too easy to capture unhurt once it gets under way. Collectors find them relatively easy to obtain, however, for they like to spend the daylight hours hiding under thin chips of rock. Frost action causes the granite boulders to exfoliate, producing thin layers of rock separated from the parent boulder, making ideal retreats for these rock-loving lizards. By prying off these semiloose flakes the creatures are uncovered and are momentarily stunned by the sudden light. But you have to grab them quickly, for they recover their wits in a hurry and go scooting away. You had better pin them down by their heads, for possibly no lizard discards its tail more readily than this one; and if you grab him by the wrong end you will most likely wind up with a wriggling tail as your only booty.

Their food consists of small beetles, millers, caterpillars, spiders, and other prey that might be abroad after sundown. In captivity, they will eat ants, flies, and mealworms but make rather unsatisfactory pets because they prefer to crawl under whatever may be in the terrarium and stay there during the day. When picked up this lizard has a curious habit of twisting its body and wrapping its tail around your finger. It can hang on very tightly and may even attempt to bite, but of course it is far too small to inflict any damage. In the fall the female gives birth to living young. Her family is small, usually only one or two.

THE SKINKS

This family (Scincidae) is the most widely distributed of any of the lizard families. We have a fair amount of representatives in this country, with many more south of our borders; but they are best represented in Australia, the East Indies, and in the Pacific Islands. The largest known species is *Tiliqua scincoides* from Australia, which attains a length of almost two feet. One of the peculiarities of this group is the differences they exhibit in the matter of legs. They may be normal in size, or they may be much reduced. The front and rear pairs may be alike or one pair may be considerably larger than the other. In some species the limbs may be lost completely, or they may be reduced far beyond the point where they might serve any useful purpose.

Our skinks are small, shiny lizards, commonly with weak legs; but they are quick in their movements and able to run with fair speed. They are characterized by smooth, rounded scales that overlap like thin shingles, imparting an almost silky appearance. Many of them burrow; and most live exclusively on the ground, only a few climbing to any extent. They seem to be able to endure cold weather better than most lizards and live further north than any other kind. In fact, if it were not for the skinks, people living in many of our northern states would never see a live lizard.

GROUND SKINK

Lygosoma laterale (Say)

This diminutive lizard has gone through a series of name changes; and in various books you will find it listed as *Leiolopisma laterale* Say, *Scincus unicolor* Harlan, or as *Leiolopisma unicolor* (Harlan). It is currently known as *Lygosoma laterale* (Say). Its popular name has not been altered, and it is still called the ground skink or sometimes the brown ground skink. Its range embraces most of eastern United States from New Jersey west through the southern sections of Ohio, Indiana, Illinois, and on to Kansas. In the South it occurs over most of central and eastern Texas and east to the Atlantic coast, including all of Florida. It enjoys possibly the widest distribution of any American lizard. It is somewhat rare in the North but very common in the South.

About four inches in length, this lizard has an elongate, cylindrical body, nearly the same size throughout, covered

Figure 68.   Ground skink.

both above and below with small smooth scales. The limbs are small and weak looking; but the tail (if not in the process of regeneration) is long and sturdy, only diminishing in size suddenly near the tip. The head is short and blunt, and the lower eyelids are provided with a tiny transparent window. The whole surface appears glossy.

The upper surface is dark chestnut in color. There is a prominent black line on each side, beginning at the snout and passing through the eye, then continuing down the side to past the middle of the tail. Sometimes there is a whitish line below the black one. There may be scattered dots of darker hue on the back. The animal is yellowish underneath, fading to white on the throat. The lower side of the tail is bluish gray.

The little brown ground skink resembles a salamander almost as much as it does a lizard. It is fond of dark, shady, and moist forests and is generally found by overturning logs or peeling the loose bark from stumps. When discovered, the creature wriggles quickly beneath a leaf or chip in an endeavor to hide. Although preferring to make its home in heavily forested regions, the ground skink is thoroughly terrestrial, never climbing into the trees but spending most of its time concealed under the debris of the forest floor. It ventures forth on brief hunting expeditions but is always ready to dart back into hiding at the first sign of danger. It feeds upon insects and their larvae, millipedes, sow bugs, and snails and is one of the few lizards that will eat earthworms. In turn it is one of the chief food items of several varieties of small snakes, particularly the scarlet snake, *Cemophora coccinea* (Blumenbach). Its habits are diurnal in the main; but it may be observed prowling at dusk and is likely to be a little more active on dull, overcast days.

This is one of the poorest of all lizards to keep for a pet. It feeds readily in captivity and is quite hardy, but it almost never stays out where you can see it. Late in June or early in July the female lays from two to five tiny eggs, commonly in the rotting wood of a stump. They hatch sometime during September.

FIVE-LINED SKINK

Eumeces fasciatus (Linne)

This, our best-known skink, is distributed over pretty nearly all of the eastern half of this country, except northern New England and the peninsula of Florida. Two closely related species replace it in the latter state; but Vermont, New Hampshire, and Maine are without lizards of any kind. Its range extends west to Texas, Oklahoma, Kansas, and the eastern sections of Nebraska and South Dakota, and throughout the Great Lakes region well into Ontario, Canada. It is much more common in the southern parts of its range.

Figure 69. Five-lined skink.

The maximum length is about nine inches; but most specimens are short of that, averaging about six inches long. The head is rather flat and pointed, and the tail is long and heavy near the body. The limbs are well developed, the fingers and toes quite long. The whole animal is encased in smooth, tightly fitting scales that impart a shiny, almost varnished appearance.

The adult stage is so unlike the juvenile form that for many years the two were regarded as separate species. Young specimens are glossy black, with a bright yellow line on the back, with two similar lines, generally narrower, on each side. The dorsal stripe forks on the head. All five lines extend to the tail, where they are lost in the most brilliant blue imaginable. In the adult stage the jet black gives way to dull brown and the stripes fade away, while the blue tail becomes brown. Females usually retain their dull stripes for life, but males become a more or less uniform olive brown. During the mating season their heads may become dull reddish. In the juvenile stage this lizard is popularly known as the blue-tailed skink, as well as the five-lined skink.

This is a secretive creature, living in shady places, commonly in forests of oak, having none of the sun-loving habits of most of the lizards. It definitely prefers moist situations but not swamps or marshes. It is a good climber and sometimes will run up a tree to escape an enemy, but it spends nearly all of its time on the ground. On bright sunny days it may be observed stretched out on a tree root or on a stone, squarely in the center of a tiny patch of sunlight that filters down through the leaves; but ordinarily one finds this lizard only by overturning flat stones or peeling the bark from rotting logs. Its habits are diurnal, but it apparently never wanders very far over the forest floor and is ever on the alert to duck under some convenient object at the first evidence of danger.

In late May the female lays from three or four up to fifteen eggs, commonly in rotting wood, such as a decaying cavity in some prostrate log or crumbling stump. The eggs are oval, white, and hard shelled and are about one-half inch long when laid; but they increase in size as the embryo develops; and by hatching time, some five or six weeks later, they are three-fourths of an inch long; and the brittle shell has become leathery. During this period the female remains with them, on guard. She is quite aggressive in defending her eggs against other lizards, including those of her own species, who would like nothing better than to make a meal of them.

This species makes a good exhibition specimen, particularly if it is a partly grown individual with its characteristic azure tail. Its chief drawback is its inherent determination to stay under something most of the time. It is a hardy lizard, not as choosey about its food as many of the others, and will generally live for a long time in captivity.

SOUTHEASTERN FIVE-LINED SKINK

Eumeces inexpectatus Taylor

This species and the next one (*laticeps*) are also five-lined when juveniles, and for some time the three five-lined skinks of the East were considered as a single species, *fasciatus*. Specialists, however, have demonstrated that there are consistent differences in the scalation of the three, and that they all deserve full specific rank. *Eumeces inexpectatus*, sometimes called the Florida five-lined skink, occupies the peninsula of Florida, even the Keys; but the name is inappropriate, because this lizard ranges north along the coastal plain all the way to Virginia. It is also found in Louisiana and over most of Mississippi but appears to be rare or absent in Alabama and in the Florida panhandle.

Figure 70. Southeastern five-lined skink.

This species grows a little larger than *fasciatus* but not very much. It has the same build, low and slim, and is just as shiny in appearance. The bright blue tail fades nearly to black as the animal grows, and the five yellowish lines that are so distinct in the young give way to an over-all brownish color in the adult stage. Like the common five-lined skink, the females may retain faint lines when fully grown.

This skink also prefers shady, moist situations and spends most of its time under stones or logs or beneath the layers of leaf-mold. It is a little more given to climbing than its northern relative and sometimes ascends trees. It is also a good swimmer, and if surprised near a pool or stream it does not hesitate to jump into the water and dive out of sight.

BROAD-HEADED SKINK

Eumeces laticeps (Schneider)

Also known as the greater five-lined skink, this is one of our largest species, sometimes reaching a total length of nearly twelve inches. Of course the average length is less than this, usually about eight inches. It occurs from southern Pennsylvania west through Ohio and Indiana to Missouri and south to eastern Texas, and its known range includes all of the southeastern states. It is much more common in the South than it is in the North.

The broad-headed skink is a robust lizard, with a large head and a thick neck, a heavy tapering tail, and sturdy limbs. Like the others, it is covered with smooth round scales that give it a polished look. There is a series of larger plates on top of the head, and the ear openings are very prominent.

Young specimens are generally uniform black above with five narrow whitish lines, the middle one larger and forking at the head. There may be a pale lateral stripe extending along the side of the head to the ear opening. The throat is yellowish, and the rest of the underside is bluish gray. The last half of the tail is a beautiful azure blue. Half-grown specimens have pale brownish streaks in the areas between the whitish lines, and the tail is slate colored. Adult males are likely to be uniform brown on the back, with no evidence of whitish lines, although they are commonly discernible in the case of adult females. Mature males have a reddish head, especially during the mating season; and "red-headed skink" is a popular name for them at this time.

The broad-headed skink seems to be pretty much restricted to wooded areas, where it lives in decaying logs and stumps and under woody debris of all sorts. Although frequently, perhaps most commonly, found on the ground, it is one of the most arboreal of any of our skinks and is often discovered well up in a tree. It is especially likely to hide in rotting cavities or under the loose bark at the forks of branches. It is not as agile as many of the scaly lizards (*Sceloporus*) are; and its climbing habits may have developed from its food habits, for one of its staple items is the bark beetle, especially the larval grubs. It also eats other insects, spiders, worms, snails, and small vertebrates such as salamanders, baby mice, tiny frogs, and other (smaller) lizards.

GREAT PLAINS SKINK

Eumeces obsoletus (Baird and Girard)

This is a lizard of the Great Plains country, being found over most of Kansas, Oklahoma, and Texas (except the Gulf Coast area). It occurs as far north as southern Nebraska, and to the west it just enters eastern Utah. It is found over most of New Mexico and Arizona, and its southern range extends well below our border. One of its popular names is Sonoran skink.

The Great Plains skink is a handsome fellow, growing to a length of about twelve inches, making it one of our largest skinks, possibly the largest. It is strong and robust in build, with a large head, thick neck, and sturdy limbs. Young specimens are black with indistinct longitudinal stripes, and their tails are bright blue. As so often has happened with creatures that differ markedly between juvenile and adult stages, the juvenile stage of this one was once considered a separate species and was named *Eumeces guttulatus*.

Figure 71.   Great Plains skink.

As the reptile grows the stripes fade; and the whole animal becomes paler in color, until eventually it takes on the adult shade of bright yellowish gray, with each scale edged in black. There may be a row or two of plain scales down the middle of the back, producing a paler band; or the whole upper surface may be covered with the black-edged scales. In any case, the skink is highly polished and most attractive in appearance. Some individuals are almost golden yellow, with a beautiful sheen. Along the sides the scales are arranged diagonally, giving the animal a characteristic pattern that is distinct from any other American skink. The underside is plain grayish white.

This lizard may be found under a variety of ecologic conditions, governed by the nature of its surroundings. On the grassy plains it occurs on hillsides, usually under flat slabs of limestone; while further west in mountainous country (it occurs up to nearly seventeen hundred feet) it is more partial to rocky situations and fallen timbers. In forested regions it can generally be found under prostrate logs along well-wooded creeks. Its habits are diurnal, but it is not very often discovered out in the open, and most specimens are obtained by overturning logs or stones.

This lizard feeds upon various insects and their larvae, spiders, and similar prey, as well as other smaller lizards and their eggs. Hard-shelled beetles are generally refused, at least in captivity. Early in the summer from six to about a dozen eggs are laid, each about five-eighths of an inch long, usually in some slight depression beneath a log or stone. The mother remains with her eggs until they hatch, late in August.

MANY-LINED SKINK

Eumeces multivirgatus (Hallowell)

The many-lined skink occurs from the southwestern corner of South Dakota through western Nebraska, the eastern part of Colorado, and in the higher regions of Arizona and New Mexico. It is a medium-sized skink, averaging about seven inches in length, with a cylindrical body, large neck, and a thick, tapering tail; but its limbs are moderately small.

The colors and markings are rather variable. Specimens from the eastern sections of its range show a strong pattern of several dark longitudinal lines on a paler ground color, with generally a marked paler streak down the center of the back; and this pale streak forks on the head. The underside is slate color and rather light in tone. Specimens from the western, more mountainous country have the numerous longitudinal lines; but they are often very indistinct.

This skink seems to get along equally well in a variety of different habitats. It lives high up on plateaus and in stony or rocky country but appears just as happy on grassy flats, where rodent burrows provide the only hiding places, and has also been taken in wooded areas. Little has been published regarding its habits, but it is known to be diurnal and presumably catches and eats the same kinds of insects that the others do. It reproduces by laying eggs.

COAL SKINK

Eumeces anthracinus (Baird)

The coal skink has a discontinuous range, being found in several widely scattered localities. The type locality (the spot from which the first specimen was obtained and described) is in Pennsylvania, and the species occurs in a broad belt extending from Lake Ontario in New York down through central Pennsylvania into northern Virginia. The species is also found in a relatively small area in central Kentucky and along the borders of Tennessee and the two Carolinas. Another colony occurs in southern Alabama. The largest area where the coal skink may be found, however, is west of the Mississippi River, where it occurs in the states of Kansas, Missouri, Arkansas, Oklahoma, and northeastern Texas.

It is a fairly stocky little skink, averaging about six inches in length, with the same general build of the group. The tail is about twice the length of the head and body, and the legs are relatively small and weak. The back is dark olive gray, glossy and iridescent. There are two narrow white lines on each side, and between them there is a broad band of coal black. The tail is colored like the back, while the limbs are darker in tone. When viewed from the side, the black color predominates, but viewing it from above, one notices first the two whitish lines that separate the broad gray back; for this reason it has been called the two-lined skink. The underside is pale bluish gray. Young specimens are frequently nearly all black, or they may show stripes like mature specimens. Their tails are deep bluish gray.

The coal skink may be found in grassy woodlands, usually in moist situations. It commonly occurs right at the edge of some swamp or creek, living under mossy logs, stones, or rotting stumps. Coal skinks are likely to be discovered under any sort of debris in such territory; and if there is open water nearby when a specimen is uncovered, it does not hesitate to jump in and dive out of sight. This skink has to be classed as a terrestrial reptile, but it shows more aquatic tendencies than possibly any of our other skinks.

PRAIRIE SKINK

Eumeces septentrionalis (Baird)

The prairie skink, as the name tells us, occurs throughout the prairie states, being found from Canada south through Minnesota and the Dakotas, as far as Kansas and northern Oklahoma. A subspecies, *obtusirostris*, extends the range south well into Texas. The species under discussion should perhaps be referred to as the northern prairie skink, and the subspecies as the southern prairie skink.

This lizard grows to a length of nearly if not fully ten inches, with the average mature specimen between seven and eight inches. Its shape is like most of the other skinks, the tail long and thick at its base, the head pointed and the

Figure 72. Prairie skink.

neck large; and the whole animal is encased in smooth, shiny, overlapping scales. The limbs are moderately robust.

Down the center of the back is a broad band of pale olive brown, and within it there may be rather weak londitudinal lines of black. Along the sides there is a narrow white line, bordered above and below by a heavy black line. A second narrow white line, again bordered by black, is usually present below. The underside is bluish gray, verging on yellowish at the chin. Young specimens sport blue tails; and during the mating season old males often become orange-red on the sides of their heads, especially on the lower jaw.

The prairie skink seems to prefer open grassland for its habitat, but there must be plenty of flat stones scattered about under which it can hide. Its distribution is somewhat spotty; and it may be relatively common in one locality and totally absent from another, even though both localities appear to be exactly alike as to soil, climate, abundance of suitable stones, etc. Its habits are diurnal, but it is such a wary creature and takes cover so quickly that practically all of the examples seen are discovered by lifting and peering under stones. Their food consists of the usual skink diet: insects and spiders, millipedes and snails, and small vertebrates. They are cannibalistic to a degree, and a large prairie skink has no qualms about eating a smaller individual of the same species.

Mating takes place in early June; and by July the female has laid about a dozen oval white eggs, each about one-half inch long. They are deposited beneath stones, or under boards and planks, and are generally placed in a shallow excavation in the soil underneath the object. They hatch in about six weeks. In the northern parts of its range the prairie skink goes into hibernation by mid-September and does not reappear again until the following May. Further south, the hibernation period is shorter. The lizards sometimes gather in large numbers to sleep away the frigid months, well below the frost line. Fifty-two have been found in one such "nest" in a gravel pit in Iowa.

WESTERN SKINK

Eumeces skiltonianus (Baird and Girard)

This is another lizard that exists as far north as Canada. It is a western species, and from British Columbia it ranges south through Washington and Oregon to western California and occurs all the way down into Mexico. It also ranges through Idaho and Nevada and the western sections of Montana and Utah. It is a reptile of stony places and can be found on the slopes of the Rocky Mountains up to an elevation of eight thousand feet. It is generally absent from the broad valleys, and of course the deserts, throughout its range.

This is a sturdy animal, with the usual skink characteristics. The limbs are moderately rugged, with five fingers and five toes, all armed with minute claws. The head is bluntly pointed with the neck somewhat swollen, and the tail is long and heavy. The lizard's length is as much as nine and one-half inches when fully grown, with the average specimen measuring about seven inches.

Figure 73. Western skink.

There is a fairly wide band of black along each side, with a narrow whitish line below it. There is also a more conspicuous whitish line above the band; and this line continues on to the snout, passing above the eye. The skink's back is light brown, smooth, and glossy. The underside is bluish gray, the throat and limbs sometimes yellowish. Young specimens have bright blue tails.

Generally speaking, this species might be termed a woods animal. Its favorite haunts are well-timbered slopes, where there is an abundance of broken rocks covering the ground. It is occasionally found on open stony hillsides but does seem to prefer shady situations. Here it may be found under stones, beneath fallen and rotting logs, or even inside hollow logs or stumps. It does its hunting during the daytime and so far as known has no nocturnal habits. It is very secretive and wary, however, like all the skinks, and will seldom be observed on the prowl. When an example is discovered, usually by overturning a log, it makes a quick dash for safety and a new hiding place; and you have to be fast in action if you are to capture it unharmed.

The western skink is noted as a burrower and frequently constructs a tunnel-like excavation a foot or more long, generally beneath a fallen log, at a depth of two or three inches. This tunnel, of course, is made in loose soil; and the lizard appears to do the job with a shovel-like motion of the snout, accompanied by a vigorous wriggling and twisting of the body, with apparently no help at all from the limbs or feet. These appendages are kept tightly folded against the body during the burrowing effort.

In late June or early July the female utilizes her burrowing abilities to hollow out a jug-shaped cavity beneath some well-embedded stone, and therein she lays from three to eight oval white eggs. Ordinarily she remains in attendance until they hatch, a matter of five or six weeks, and for a short period of a day or two thereafter; and then the youngsters are left entirely to their own resources. Their survival and ultimate growth is dependent upon their individual alertness and luck.

GREATER BROWN SKINK

Eumeces gilberti Van Denburgh

Sometimes known as the greater western skink, this is a really big fellow, possibly our largest skink. It attains a maximum length of about twelve inches, although the average example is between seven and nine. It is a strong and rugged lizard, with a large head, sturdy limbs, and a thick, heavy tail. It is found in northern Arizona and southern Utah and in east central California but appears to be absent from Nevada, which lies between these two regions. A subspecies, *rubricaudatus*, occurs south through central California into Mexico.

Young specimens are marked with longitudinal lines, a pair of pale ones just off the center of the back, and another along each side, each pale line edged with black. The tail is blue, and the underside is slate colored. By the time the youngster is a little more than half grown the tail loses its bright color and becomes dull brown, and the longitudinal

Figure 74. Greater brown skink.

lines begin to fade out. When fully grown, the lizard shows little or no evidence of lines at all; and its whole back is uniform in color, a sort of brownish olive. The head and neck become brick red, and in males the head is often greatly swollen at the rear of the jaws.

The greater brown skink is perhaps most common in stony or rocky country, on the slopes of the mountains, but is also found on grasslands if there are a goodly number of hiding places available, such as rodent burrows and scattered boulders. Its habits are diurnal, and its food is largely made up of the insects that share the territory. Like many of our sizeable lizards, this one will bite occasionally when first captured; but it is not large enough to cause any worry; and as a rule it calms down rather quickly and makes a satisfactory pet.

SAND SKINK

Neoseps reynoldsi Stejneger

This is a peculiar lizard, quite different from any other species in this country. It is long and slender, with four legs that are so tiny that they are of no practical use to the reptile. The rear pair are thin and weak but at least noticeable, while the front pair are so small that they border on the ridiculous; in fact, you have to look sharply in order to see them at all. The front feet have degenerated to a single claw, while there are two claws on each hind foot. The skink is nearly five inches long, half of which is a robust tail that is the same size nearly to its tip, where it abruptly tapers to a point. The head is small and pointed, the snout shovel-like. The animal has eyelids, the lower ones provided with a transparent "window," but there are no external ear openings.

The sand skink ranges through central and southern Florida. Its color is light brown above and slate-color below. On the back there is a pair of tiny dark spots on each scale, giving the lizard an all-over dotted appearance. There is a darker stripe along the side of the head, and this continues as an indistinct line down the side.

As you might guess from its general build, the sand skink is a burrowing animal; or, as the scientists would say, its habits are fossorial. It is not likely to be found in moist situations but prefers living in relatively dry territory with loose sandy soil. Here it occurs under logs and other objects; but your chances of finding a specimen are not too hopeful, as only a few have ever been found. Occasional specimens have turned up during sand-sifting operations, some from a depth of more than two feet; and others have been discovered while excavating for one purpose or another. They have been obtained by simply overturning logs in some sandy scrub-pine area, but this species certainly has to be classed as a rare lizard.

As might be inferred from the above, extremely little is known about the habits and the natural history of this species. Presumably it feeds upon insects, and it is believed to reproduce by laying eggs. The long and heavy tail is lost rather easily. A fine, adult, complete example of the sand skink would be a prize indeed for any young collector of reptiles in Florida.

SIX-LINED RACERUNNER

Cnemidophorus sexlineatus (Linne)

The racerunner, as its name implies, is an active, energetic lizard, noted for its speed in getting over the ground when in a hurry. It enjoys a very wide distribution, occurring from West Virginia and Maryland to Florida, where it is found throughout the state. Westward, it ranges across the country as far as southeastern Wyoming and central Texas and northward to Wisconsin and Minnesota. Throughout this whole territory there are no subspecies recognized.

The racerunner is a trimly built lizard, growing to a length of about ten inches. It has a very long, tapering tail;

Figure 75.   Six-lined racerunner.

and its limbs are relatively long and slender, with long fingers and toes, all terminating in sharp claws. The tongue is forked like a snake's and is frequently flicked out in the same manner. The body color is some shade of brown; and there are six yellowish stripes running the length of the back, starting at the top of the head behind the eyes and ending at the base of the tail. At the sides, the longitudinal stripes continue part way down the tail. In addition, there is usually a broader, pale-brownish band extending from just back of the head to the tail. In females the underside is whitish, but with males considerable areas of the ventral surface are bright blue, and the lower parts of the limbs may be yellowish.

The six-lined racerunner is a ground-loving species, seldom showing any inclination to climb. Throughout its wide range it is to be found under many different conditions; but in general it seems to prefer dry, sandy situations and is often seen along the borders of dirt roads out in the country. It runs over the ground with an uneven, jerky motion; but when thoroughly frightened it can travel at a bewildering rate of speed, almost too fast to follow with the eye when it is dashing away through sparse grass. The long tail is dragged in the dirt when the animal is not hurrying; but when really under way it is held out stiffly behind, and probably acts as a sort of balance.

It goes without saying that this lizard is rather hard to catch, alive and unhurt. Fortunately for collectors, however, it usually does not run very far but soon ducks under a stone or disappears in some shallow ground hole and in most cases is not very difficult to dig out. Throughout much of its range it is likely to use the burrows of rodents and moles for hideaways, although it is capable of digging its own retreats, and sometimes does just that, scratching away energetically in the loose soil.

When the weather is warm these lizards are active quite early in the morning and may be seen scurrying about among the grasses and pebbles in search of food. They continue being active until late afternoon, when they usually seek resting places, and by sundown it is generally hard to find a specimen abroad. They sleep during the night and bright and early the next morning are on the job again. They are not likely to be seen on dull, overcast days; and of course they keep well hidden during rainy weather.

Insects make up most of their food, supplemented by spiders and snails. Moths, butterflies, ants, flies, grasshoppers, crickets, and various grubs and caterpillars are taken; but beetles of the hard-shelled kind are not high on the preferred list, although they are eaten occasionally. One observer reports watching a specimen take a ladybird beetle and promptly spit it out, after which the lizard rubbed its mouth vigorously in the dirt. Apparently, that particular kind of beetle is distasteful to the racerunner!

Throughout most of its range the racerunner hibernates during the winter, commonly in some burrow well below the frostline, and mating takes place soon after the lizards have appeared in the spring. During June the female lays about a half-dozen oval eggs, each white, hard-shelled, and about one-half inch long. The eggs are concealed underground, usually in a shallow pit beneath some stone or log.

The racerunner often uses mole burrows for this purpose, constructing small side-galleries off the main tunnel. The eggs hatch in about six weeks.

The six-lined racerunner makes an excellent exhibition specimen. The species is common enough so that it is not hard to obtain an example or to replace one that may have been injured in capture and did not live very long. It is a lively, wide-awake lizard, not likely to try to keep out of sight most of the time. It is not at all bashful about eating and will take mealworms or flies from your fingers in no time at all. It is a reasonably hardy reptile, and if kept in a dry cage in a warm place (but not directly in the sun all day) it should live contentedly for a long time.

CHECKERED WHIPTAIL

Cnemidophorus tessellatus (Say)

The checkered whiptail, or racerunner, is found from Oregon and Idaho south through Nevada, California, Utah, New Mexico, and Arizona. It just gets into southwestern Colorado and ranges well down into Mexico. Some ten inches in length, of which the tail constitutes two-thirds, this is another rugged but streamlined lizard; and you have only to look at it to know it is built for speed.

The general color is gray with black markings. There are three rows of irregular black spots down the back, starting back of the head and continuing on the tail, with narrow lines of the gray ground color between them. A series of black spots on the sides runs the other way, transversely, and these often merge with each other in a way to produce bars. Broken spotting is present on the neck and the sides of the face, and the limbs are covered with smaller black dots. There is a fair amount of variation, however, and some individuals will be more spotted and barred than others. The underside is slate-gray, more or less marbled and dotted with black.

Figure 76. Checkered whiptail.

The checkered whiptail is at home under a variety of conditions but prefers dry, hard-packed soil and open deserts or flatlands as a rule. Specimens have been found on plateaus some seven thousand feet in altitude, and they occur in some of the California deserts that are below sea level. Rock-strewn canyon bottoms are perhaps their favorite locations. Like many of the desert inhabitants, this one is most active during the morning hours; and by the time the sun has reached its zenith, and for the rest of the early afternoon, the checkered whiptail lizards have all gone into hiding, either resting in the shade of a cactus or underground in a rodent burrow. Later there may be another period of activity.

Like all of the whiptails or racerunners, this one is a speedy lizard, extremely hard to catch. It is alert and wary, and long before you can get close it takes off for other parts. It is strictly a ground lizard and is not known to climb into bushes or shrubs; however, it will scale a large boulder with ease and dispatch. When running away from an enemy this species is a real expert in keeping a cactus or mesquite bush between itself and the pursuer. In most cases, when alarmed, it will head for the nearest shrub; and once behind that will hesitate for a second and then go streaking off at an angle to the next shrub, and so on. The best method of collecting a live specimen is to press the pursuit until eventually the tiring lizard takes refuge in a burrow that can be dug up or beneath a stone that is not too large to turn over.

SPOTTED WHIPTAIL

Cnemidophorus sacki Wiegmann

This lizard is found in New Mexico, Arizona, and in the southern parts of Utah and Colorado. To the south its range extends well down into Mexico. A subspecies, *gularis,* occupies most of Texas, a good portion of Oklahoma, and the southeastern corner of New Mexico, so that the spotted whiptail may be said to occur over most of the Southwest, although it does not get as far west as southern California. It is a sizeable lizard, attaining a length of better than ten inches, and has the same racy but sturdy build of all the racerunners.

The color is dark gray above, with six paler lines running from the head to the base of the tail. Between these light

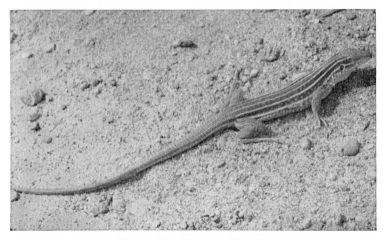

Figure 77.   Spotted whiptail.

lines, on the broader dark areas, are a number of small whitish dots, evenly spaced. These characteristic dots are not present in young specimens. The dark (spotted) stripe along the side usually continues part way on the tail. On the ventral surface the females are pale yellowish white, while the males' underparts are more inclined to bluish white.

The spotted whiptail prefers hot and dry country, where the land is relatively flat and the vegetation sparse and spiny. It is strictly terrestrial and diurnal in habits, being most active during the morning hours and generally resting in the late afternoon. The lizards scurry about among the cactus and other desert plants with a jerky and uneven gait, scratching and groveling in the debris, ever on the search for something to eat. Ants and other insects make up most of their food. It is capable of rapid movement when necessary and can run like a gray streak when frightened. It is not as wary as many of the whiptail group, however, and will usually permit a person to approach to within a few feet before it takes off. It is likely to run no more than a dozen feet before it stops abruptly and turns around to see if it is being followed.

The spotted whiptail lays from eight to ten white eggs in the early summer, which are generally buried in loose soil at a depth of two or three inches. A favorite place is in a shallow excavation under the fallen trunk of a Joshua tree. The eggs hatch in the late summer, and at first the little whiptails look very much like six-lined racerunners; the spots begin to appear between the longitudinal lines when they are partly grown.

ARIZONA WHIPTAIL

Cnemidophorus stictogrammus Lowe

The Arizona whiptail is one of the largest members of its genus in this country, growing to a length of about twelve inches over-all, with its tail making up considerably more

Figure 78. Arizona whiptail.

than half. It occurs in Arizona and parts of neighboring
New Mexico. The classification of the genus *Cnemidophorus*
is still far from completely settled. Some herpetologists
consider *stictogrammus* a subspecies of *sacki*, while others
believe it is entitled to specific rank. There is so much variation within the group, and many of the species are so
plastic, that those from one kind of terrain are not always
the same as those from another. Practically every specialist
has, at one time or another, stated that this is the most difficult group in American herpetology. They give the experts
real trouble. What one worker believes to be a good species
is regarded by another worker as a variety or subspecies of
something else, while some equally capable student of the
group may declare it to be a subspecies of an entirely different species. Eventually, as more and more material is collected and evaluated, some stability will be achieved; but it
must be admitted that as of right now, there is considerable
uncertainty as to the status of several varieties of the whiptail lizards.

The Arizona whiptail is dark gray above and white below. There is a distinct pale stripe along each side, and two

more on the back, well over toward the sides. Down the center of the back are three lines of rounded dots, so closely spaced and regular that they suggest knobby lines; and between all of these longitudinal lines, on a background of gray that is so dark it is almost black, are regularly spaced whitish spots. The tail is unspotted, but the limbs are pale gray above with numerous white spots.

This big lizard is a speedy traveler when so inclined and is a hard fellow to catch alive and unhurt. It is, however, not as quickly frightened as some of the racerunners and as a rule will permit you to get fairly close before it shows any signs of alarm. Its favorite haunts are on the open desert floor, amid the cactus and other prickly plants, where it forages for ants, beetles, grasshoppers, and similar prey. It is most active from shortly after sunup until a little past noon, and in the afternoon is likely to be found resting in the shade of some desert plant, beneath a fallen limb or branch of some kind, or just inside the entrance of a rodent burrow.

WESTERN WHIPTAIL

Cnemidophorus tigris Baird and Girard

This species is found in the valleys of central Utah. There are no less than seven subspecies recognized, more than with any other of our racerunners, so that the western whiptail, in one of its forms, can be said to occur over a rather wide territory in the West. It is a trimly built reptile, sturdy and strong, which attains a length of about ten inches.

The predominant color is gray. There are several pale stripes running the full length of the body, from just back of the head to the base of the tail; and between these longitudinal lines are broader bands of deep gray, liberally spotted with light gray dots. The spots on the sides are often so arranged that the dark areas between them tend to form transverse bars. The limbs are mottled and speckled with gray and white; and the ventral surface varies from white to pale gray, generally much darker on the chest and throat.

Figure 79.   Western whiptail.

The western whiptail, sometimes called the tiger whiptail or tiger racerunner, is another lizard that seems to thrive in hot and dry territory. It is at home in the broad valleys of sandy wastelands, where it may be seen scooting about amid the prickly vegetation in a jerky, hesitant fashion. When unduly alarmed, however, it can take off in a flash; and it is just as speedy as any of the other racerunners. Its habits are diurnal, and the best time to find specimens abroad is during the morning hours.

The western whiptail reproduces by laying eggs. They number from six to eight and are buried in shallow excavations in the soil, commonly under some object. They hatch in from four to six weeks.

Like most of the whiptails, this one is no climber. It can scale the stony face of a boulder with no trouble at all and is perfectly capable of climbing into the branches of the mesquite and sage and other shrubs of its neighborhood, but it seems to prefer staying on the ground. It usually rests during the hottest part of the day in rodent burrows or beneath stones or bark. One specimen that the author has insists on making its home under the water dish in its cage. There are plenty of stones and pieces of bark scattered about; but it always burrows in the sand under the glass dish, even though the dish is moved from place to place every few days. Possibly the water overhead produces some cooling effect the lizard enjoys.

This lizard feeds almost exclusively upon insects (and spiders) and has been observed operating in a manner that reminds one of a foraging chicken. It will scratch industrially in the earth around the roots of plants, using its front feet only; and after it has disturbed a fair amount of sand or soil it will back up a little and snap up ants and other tiny insects with rapid darts of its head.

CALIFORNIA ALLIGATOR LIZARD

Gerrhonotus coeruleus Wiegmann

The alligator lizards, so called because of their general build, long snouts, and heavy scales, do remind one of miniature editions of the big saurians of our southern swamps; yet when you place a baby alligator beside an alligator lizard of the same size they do not look at all alike. There are five species in this country, with more than a dozen subspecies; and the group is found in Texas, Arizona, and along the Pacific coast from British Columbia all the way down to Baja California.

The California alligator lizard is found along the coastal area in central California. In northern California it is replaced by the closely allied subspecies *shastensis* Fitch, while north of that state the subspecies *principis* (Baird and Girard) occupies a large area extending north into British Columbia and eastward through Idaho to central Montana.

This is a solid and rugged lizard, growing to a length of more than one foot. The head is somewhat elongate, swelling a little at the snout; the limbs are sturdy and strong; and the tail is about twice the length of the rest of the animal. The tail is rather large and thick for about half its length, then tapers gradually to a fine point. The scales are large and shiny, so that the reptile appears to be fitted into a suit

Figure 80.   California alligator lizard.

of armor. One of the older popular names for these creatures is "plaited lizards."

The color is olive gray above, verging on greenish, with
about a dozen dark blotches on the back that tend to form
crossbands. The sides are darker, with numerous white
specks arranged in an irregular fashion but commonly sug-
gesting vertical lines. The limbs and tail are plainly barred,
and the lizard's underside is whitish.

This species is found in cooler and moderately humid
country, commonly in pine forests. It is active during the
daylight hours, traveling about in an almost serpentine manner. It moves slowly, and the shiny body and long tail follow the bumps and hollows of the ground; and although the
legs are busy all the time, the effect resembles a gliding
movement. Its progress over uneven ground is suggestive
of the locomotion of the completely legless "glass snake," a
lizard to be described later; and it is easy to see why scientists place them both in the same family (Anguidae).

The food of this lizard largely consists of beetles, grass-hoppers, grubs, ants, and other relatively slow-moving insects. Spiders and snails are consumed, and occasionally the alligator lizard will capture and devour a small vertebrate or rob a bird's nest. Van Denburgh reported that young specimens, after successfully capturing an insect, held it firmly in their jaws while they rolled rapidly over and over, grinding the insect in the sand. This interesting habit of rapidly rotating the body while holding the limbs and tail stiffly back is a device developed by the alligators and crocodiles for tearing parts from larger bodies, but they perform this act in the water. Large alligator lizards are said to sometimes grab hold of a piece of your skin and go into this "spin," and it can be quite painful! The author has had alligator lizards of two species in his care for a period of six months and has never witnessed this act, but animals in captivity often fail to display the same traits that they do in a wild state.

Alligator lizards have the ability to part with their tails at the slightest provocation. This habit is common with nearly all lizards, but with these reptiles the animal is able to snap it off voluntarily by a sudden twist as it is running for shelter. The operation is a bloodless one; and the cast-off tail wriggles and thrashes about violently for several seconds, thus distracting the enemy. A new tail eventually replaces the discarded one, but it never grows as long as the original appendage. This habit is so prevalent with the alligator lizards that in a day's collecting, specimens with perfect tails are very likely to be in the minority.

ARIZONA ALLIGATOR LIZARD

Gerrhonotus kingi (Gray)

The Arizona alligator lizard is found in central and southern Arizona, southwestern New Mexico, and over much of central Mexico. It is a large species, attaining a length of at least twelve inches. Its general build is about the same as *coeruleus,* the species just described; but its limbs are smaller and weaker. The scales on its back are feebly keeled.

This species is strongly banded on its back, the bands continuing all the way to the tip of the tail. The ground color above is ashy gray, crossed by more or less wavy bands of nearly black. The bands extend down over the sides, where they are narrowed and somewhat flecked with white. The limbs are commonly barred, and the head is mottled gray and black. The underside is uniform gray.

Because of its shorter legs, the movements of this lizard are even more snakelike in appearance than those of the last species. It seems to be slow and awkward in getting over the ground; but collectors report that it is not an easy lizard to capture alive and in good shape, especially with a full-sized tail. It roams about in the daytime and is strictly terrestrial in habits.

In general, this lizard is more abundant at higher elevations and is to be looked for on plateaus and in mountain valleys. The terrain does not seem to matter very much, for they are equally at home in grasslands, in wooded areas, on gravelly sand flats with sparse vegetation, or in stony canyons.

GLASS "SNAKE"

Ophisaurus ventralis (Linne)

The glass "snake" is not a snake at all but a legless lizard which is found in our Southern and Western states. In the East it ranges from Virginia to Florida; but in the Middle West it ventures further north, occurring from Texas to Nebraska and Wisconsin. There are three very closely related forms, which for many years have been considered a single species, *Ophisaurus ventralis.* Now a more slender form from the Middle West has been recognized and named *O. attenuatus,* with a subspecies, *longicaudus,* occurring more toward the east. All have the same habits and are almost identical in appearance.

Figure 81. Glass "snake."

With its elongate, serpentine body, and complete lack of legs, it is small wonder that the name "snake" has been attached to this reptile. It has several characteristics, however, that immediately separate it from the serpents and place it among the lizards. Well-developed eyelids and ear openings, which no snakes possess; a broad tongue; and small overlapping scales on the belly instead of broad plates are some of the distinguishing characteristics that are plainly visible at a glance. Let us call these interesting creatures by their right name: glass lizards.

The largest glass lizard ever measured was thirty-seven and one-half inches long, but the average specimen is about two feet in length. The upper surface is olive or greenish brown, with many dots of bright green on each scale. The lower surface is uniform pale green. On many individuals the dots along the sides run together in a manner that suggests narrow greenish stripes, especially noticeable on the neck.

The whole lizard is very shiny and presents a "glassy" appearance; but the term "glass snake" refers to the creature's apparent ability to break up into several pieces when struck with a stick, which, unfortunately, is the usual fate of almost any snake-like animal that has the bad luck to come into contact with man. What happens, of course, is that the tail is loosely attached to the body, as is the case with so many of the lizards; and since this species has a very long tail and no limbs, the animal appears to break in two near the middle; furthermore, the discarded tail itself may break into two or more sections. There is no bleeding, and the "man with a stick" may well believe he has shattered the "serpent." According to folklore, the "snake" would reassemble itself if left alone and be as good as new. The abandoned tail, however, is gone forever and if left until doomsday will not join up with the body again. If the creature has been fortunate enough to escape while the man was belaboring the squirming tail, it will promptly start growing a new caudal appendage and in a few weeks will indeed be nearly as good as ever, although the new tail is seldom as long as the original.

The glass lizard is probably diurnal to a large extent, although it is known to be abroad occasionally at night. It may be found in grassy and weedy places, perhaps most frequently in the neighborhood of streams or around the borders of ponds. It is probable that the lizard finds better hunting in such places, rather than having any preference for moist or swampy situations; and yet specimens are said to be most abundant following rains.

It does a considerable amount of burrowing, and individuals are now and then turned out while plowing or when harvesting sweet potatoes. Above ground it is rather stiff and awkward, lacking the graceful movements of a serpent; but even so it is capable of traveling at a respectable rate of speed. When held in the hand it twists and turns its body in an effort to escape, and as the scales rub together they make a creaking sound. Freshly caught specimens, especially large ones, will generally attempt to bite; but in captivity they become very gentle and can be taught to take food from the fingers.

In a wild state the glass lizard feeds upon spiders, insects, grubs, and snails. It likes to burrow underneath the leaf mold along stream courses, and when the lizard chances upon a salamander or small snake it promptly devours this prey. It is very fond of birds' eggs, which it crushes and then laps up the contents with its broad tongue. In captivity it does well on mealworms, grasshoppers, crickets, and beetles; but it may turn cannibalistic if several individuals of varying size are kept in the same cage.

FOOTLESS LIZARD

Anniella pulchra Gray

This is another limbless lizard, found on our West Coast. It occurs from central California down into Baja California. The glass lizard (*Ophisaurus*) just described has well-developed eyes and ears. This genus, which is the only one in its family, has functional eyes but no ears.

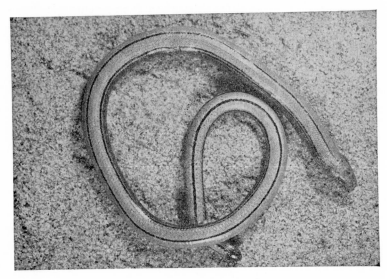

Figure 82. Footless lizard.

It is a small, wormlike creature, seldom more than seven inches long. Its diameter is about one-quarter of an inch, and it is quite blunt at both ends. Tiny polished scales cover the body, top and bottom; and you have to look closely to determine which end is the front and which is the back. The head is small, with a tiny mouth and very small eyes, which have lids.

The color above is silvery olive, with a dark brown or black line down the center of the back, from just back of the head to the end of the tail. There is a conspicuous dark area at the tail tip, adding to the confusion as to which end is which, for from a little distance the darker end looks as if it should be the head. The underside is yellowish. A much darker form, sometimes nearly purplish, occurs in a restricted area in central California and has been named as a subspecies, *Anniella pulchra nigra* Fischer.

The footless lizard is a burrower, as you would certainly guess. It seems to be at home in various habitats, both open grasslands and wooded areas; but the soil must be loose and preferably somewhat sandy near the surface and damp further down. Most authorities agree that moisture is essential to the well-being of these creatures, and they are not to be found ordinarily in arid or semiarid country. Apparently these lizards do not appear on the surface of the ground very often and are very likely to be most active late in the afternoon.

Their food is made up chiefly of small insects and larvae that they find as they burrow beneath the grass roots and litter of leaves under bushes and shrubs. The lizard moves rather stiffly above ground, and it is plain to see that *pulchra* is more at home just below the surface. A specimen turned out by raking the debris under a board or log will lose no time in getting back underground.

The footless lizard does not lay eggs but gives birth to living young. This generally takes place in the fall; and the broods are small, usually no more than four or five at a time, and frequently only one.

GILA MONSTER

Heloderma suspectum Cope

Let us begin the discussion of this interesting reptile by pronouncing its name correctly. Many Spanish words sound quite different from the way they look when set in type. In this one, the "G" is pronounced like an "H"; and the right pronunciation for this lizard is "heela" monster. It is the only poisonous lizard found in this country, occurring from southern Utah and Nevada to southern Arizona and New Mexico. A closely related species lives south of the border in Mexico, and these two constitute the only known poisonous lizards in the world.

The average length of an adult gila monster is about eighteen inches, and a specimen that attains a length of two feet is a real giant. The body is stout, with short stubby limbs; the head is large, blunt, and rounded; and the tail is short and fat. The tongue is broad and fleshy and is forked at its tip. In place of scales, the body is covered with rounded tubercles, or points, so that the lizard appears to be adorned with a suit of round glass beads.

Figure 83. Gila monster.

The colors are variable, but the animal is always strikingly marked. The entire beast, below as well as above, is marbled with coal black and some other hue, which is commonly salmon, but may be pink, yellow, or even white. The lizard's back has often been likened to the pattern of a Navajo blanket. The limbs and feet are usually black, and the sides of the head and the lower jaw are black. The tail has three or four broad black bands, with spots in the colored areas between them.

As one might infer from its build, this is a sluggish, slow-moving creature most of the time. It seldom lifts its body off the ground but drags itself along in a deliberate manner. At the same time, it can raise up when it has to defend itself and is capable of turning quickly and snapping with agility that would do credit to a dog. So take no chances with these fellows that look so slow and helpless. It hisses loudly when tormented, and once it succeeds in getting a secure hold on the enemy it hangs on with the tenacity of a bulldog, and a strong set of fingers is needed to break its hold without something to pry with. Like the snapping turtle, the gila monster's head may be severed from its body and the jaws will retain their viselike grip.

There has been considerable controversy as to just how venomous this big lizard really is. Some authorities claim its bite is very dangerous and potentially even fatal, and others maintain with equal vigor that its bite is no more harmful than that of a small dog. There is ample evidence of persons being bitten and suffering no ill effects whatsoever, but this can be easily explained. The creature's poison glands are embedded in the lower jaw, one on each side; and the grooved teeth that introduce the venom into a wound are situated well back in the reptile's mouth. The gila monster needs to get a full grip and then "chew" in order to inject its poison successfully. This the lizard tries its best to do whenever it gets the chance; but a superficial nip or even a good healthy bite, if broken quickly, would very probably fail to inject any venom; and the bitten person would therefore be firmly convinced that the gila monster had been greatly overestimated as a dangerous animal. However, its venom injected into a small mammal kills it as quickly as if it had been bitten by a poisonous snake, and there are plenty of cases on record where the lizard's bite has produced serious results in man. Competent herpetologists are unanimous in the opinion that the gila monster can be a very dangerous reptile. The grooved teeth, mentioned earlier, bear a groove on the front and on the back, the one on the front larger. There is no apparatus for forcing the venom through these grooves, like the hypodermic arrangement of the pit vipers, the grooves merely providing convenient channels through which the venom may flow into the wound.

The gila monster is an inhabitant of flat desert valleys and broad canyon bottoms, spending the hot daylight hours resting under rocks or in burrows and prowling mostly after sundown. In such dry and inhospitable country, it seems strange that so heavy and slow an animal can manage to get enough food to stay alive. It is known to eat insects, centipedes, and lizards and is very fond of eggs. In the wild it no doubt finds and devours many lizards' and snakes' eggs and has been observed climbing laboriously into prickly bushes in order to rob birds' nests. Its huge tail serves as a reservoir for the storage of fat, and when hunting is good it becomes tremendously stout. During periods of scarcity the reptile is able to exist, even for months, on the fat thus stored up. It is believed to estivate during the hottest part of the season.

In a wild state the gila monster is bad tempered and vicious but after a few days in captivity becomes one of the most docile of all reptiles and will permit almost any amount of rough handling without showing any signs of resentment. However, no one should ever take unnecessary chances, or get the least bit careless, when dealing with an animal that can be dangerous. Many keepers at zoos have noted that when you take the most gentle of gila monsters from its cage and put it in the bright sun for a short time, it reverts to its original savage disposition and quick actions. A strange behavior trait with captive specimens is their love for water.

In a wild state they probably seldom even see any water; and we commonly think of them as ideal dwellers of hot, scorchingly dry country. In captivity they will climb into their water dish if possible; and if it is large enough they will soak in it for days at a time, all but their heads completely submerged.

About the only food they will accept in captivity is hens' eggs. They rarely ever bother any other animal placed in their cage and will permit lizards, baby mice, and fat grasshoppers to crawl all over them without seeming to realize that according to the book they are supposed to eat such things. Two fine adults in the author's possession consume four well-beaten eggs once a week. The eggs are placed in a small dish, and the reptiles lap them up with their broad tongues. Gila monsters have been known to live in captivity for nearly twenty years, on a steady diet of raw eggs.

In late July, the female lays from five or six up to a dozen large, soft-shelled eggs. They average about two and one-half inches in length and are deposited in a shallow excavation that she scrapes out in the sand, preferably in some moist place, such as close by a creek in some canyon bottom. The eggs hatch in about five weeks, the little gila monsters being some four inches long. They are marked like their parents, only more vividly.

There are only two species in this genus, and the other one occurs in Mexico. This is the Mexican beaded lizard, *Heloderma horridum* (Wiegmann), known to the natives of that country as the "Silatica." It grows to a slightly larger size than our gila monster and has a much longer tail. It is black and yellow in color, with the black predominating; the head is entirely black, whereas the head of our species is marbled on top like the body. Both species are equally poisonous.

CLASSIFICATION OF THE REPTILES DISCUSSED IN THIS BOOK

Kingdom: ANIMAL

Phylum: CHORDATA

Class: REPTILIA

Order: CHELONIA

Suborder: THECOPHORA

Family: KINOSTERNIDAE

Sternotherus odoratus (Musk Turtle)
Sternotherus carinatus (Mississippi Musk Turtle)
Kinosternon subrubrum (Mud Turtle)
Kinosternon bauri (Striped Mud Turtle)
Kinosternon flavescens (Yellow Mud Turtle)
Kinosternon flavescens spooneri (Illinois Mud Turtle)

Family: CHELYDRIDAE

Chelydra serpentina (Snapping Turtle)
Macrochelys temmincki (Alligator Snapping Turtle)

Family: EMYDIDAE

Clemmys guttata (Spotted Turtle)
Clemmys muhlenbergi (Muhlenberg's Turtle)
Clemmys marmorata (Pacific Pond Turtle)
Clemmys insculpta (Wood Turtle)
Emys blandingi (Blanding's Turtle)
Terrapene carolina (Box Turtle)
Terrapene carolina bauri (Florida Box Turtle)
Terrapene carolina major (Gulf Coast Box Turtle)
Terrapene carolina triunguis (Three-toed Box Turtle)
Terrapene ornata (Ornate Box Turtle)

Malaclemys terrapin (Diamondback Terrapin)
Malaclemys terrapin centrata (Southern Diamondback Terrapin)
Malaclemys terrapin macrospilota (Florida Diamondback Terrapin)
Malaclemys terrapin pileata (Mississippi Diamondback Terrapin)
Malaclemys terrapin rhizophorarum (Mangrove Diamondback
  Terrapin)
Malaclemys terrapin littoralis (Texas Diamondback Terrapin)
Graptemys barbouri (Barbour's Sawback Turtle)
Graptemys geographica (Map Turtle)
Graptemys pseudogeographica (False Map Turtle)
Graptemys pseudogeographica kohni (Kohn's False Map Turtle)
Chrysemys picta (Painted Turtle)
Chrysemys picta marginata (Midland Painted Turtle)
Chrysemys picta dorsalis (Southern Painted Turtle)
Chrysemys picta belli (Western Painted Turtle)
Pseudemys floridana (Coastal Plain Turtle)
Pseudemys floridana concinna (River Turtle)
Pseudemys floridana hieroglyphica (Hieroglyphic Turtle)
Pseudemys floridana peninsularis (Peninsular Turtle)
Pseudemys floridana suwanniensis (Suwannee Turtle)
Pseudemys floridana mobiliensis (Mobile Turtle)
Pseudemys floridana hoyi (Saw-tooth Slider)
Pseudemys floridana texana (Texas Slider)
Pseudemys rubriventris (Red-bellied Turtle)
Pseudemys rubriventris bangsi (Plymouth Turtle)
Pseudemys nelsoni (Florida Red-bellied Turtle)
Pseudemys scripta (Yellow-bellied Turtle)
Pseudemys scripta elegans (Red-eared Turtle)
Deirochelys reticularia (Chicken Turtle)

FAMILY: TESTUDINIDAE

Gopherus polyphemus (Gopher Tortoise)
Gopherus berlandieri (Texas Gopher Tortoise)
Gopherus agassizi (Desert Tortoise)

FAMILY: TRIONYCHIDAE

Trionyx ferox (Southern Soft-shelled Turtle)
Trionyx ferox agassizi (Carolina Soft-shelled Turtle)
Trionyx ferox aspera (Gulf Coast Soft-shelled Turtle)
Trionyx ferox emoryi (Texas Soft-shelled Turtle)

Trionyx ferox spinifera (Eastern Soft-shelled Turtle)
Trionyx ferox hartwegi (Western Soft-shelled Turtle)
Trionyx muticus (Smooth Soft-shelled Turtle)

FAMILY: CHELONIIDAE

Chelonia mydas (Green Turtle)
Caretta caretta (Loggerhead Turtle)
Eretmochelys imbricata (Hawksbill Turtle)
Lepidochelys kempi (Ridley Turtle)

FAMILY: DERMOCHELIDAE

Dermochelys coriacea (Leatherback Turtle)

ORDER: SQUAMATA

SUBORDER: LACERTILIA

FAMILY: GEKKONIDAE

Gonatodes fuscus (Yellow-headed Gecko)
Hemidactylus turcicus (Mediterranean Gecko)
Sphaerodactylus cinereus (Ashy Gecko)
Sphaerodactylus notatus (Reef Gecko)
Phyllodactylus tuberculosus (Leaf-footed Gecko)
Coleonyx variegatus (Desert Banded Gecko)
Coleonyx brevis (Texas Banded Gecko)

FAMILY: IGUANIDAE

Anolis carolinensis (Carolina Anole)
Anolis stejnegeri (Key West Anole)
Anolis sagrei (Cuban Brown Anole)
Dipsosaurus dorsalis (Desert Iguana)
Sauromalus obesus (Chuckwalla)
Holbrookia maculata (Northern Earless Lizard)
Holbrookia texana (Texas Earless Lizard)
Holbrookia propinqua (Keeled Earless Lizard)
Callisaurus draconoides gabbi (Zebra-tailed Lizard)
Uma notata (Colorado Desert Fringe-toed Lizard)
Uma notata inornata (Coachella Valley Fringe-toed Lizard)
Crotaphytus collaris (Collared Lizard)
Crotaphytus collaris baileyi (Bailey's Collared Lizard)

Crotaphytus wislizeni (Leopard Lizard)
Sceloporus undulatus (Fence Lizard)
Sceloporus undulatus hyacinthinus (Northern Fence Lizard)
Sceloporus undulatus elongatus (Northern Plateau Lizard)
Sceloporus undulatus garmani (Northern Prairie Lizard)
Sceloporus undulatus consobrinus (Southern Prairie Lizard)
Sceloporus undulatus tristichus (Southern Plateau Lizard)
Sceloporus occidentalis (Northwestern Fence Lizard)
Sceloporus occidentalis biseriatus (San Joaquin Fence Lizard)
Sceloporus woodi (Florida Scrub Lizard)
Sceloporus graciosus (Sagebrush Lizard)
Sceloporus graciosus gracilis (California Sagebrush Lizard)
Sceloporus olivaceus (Texas Spiny Lizard)
Sceloporus magister (Desert Spiny Lizard)
Sceloporus clarki (Clark's Spiny Lizard)
Sceloporus jarrovi (Yarrow's Spiny Lizard)
Sceloporus poinsetti (Crevice Spiny Lizard)
Uta graciosus (Long-tailed Brush Lizard)
Uta ornata (Texas Tree Lizard)
Uta stansburiana (Side-blotched Lizard)
Uta mearnsi (Banded Rock Lizard)
Phrynosoma cornutum (Texas Horned Lizard)
Phrynosoma platyrhinos (Desert Horned Lizard)
Phrynosoma coronatum blainvillei (San Diego Horned Lizard)
Phrynosoma coronatum frontale (California Horned Lizard)
Phrynosoma douglasi (Short-horned Lizard)

FAMILY: XANTUSIIDAE

Xantusia vigilis (Desert Night Lizard)
Xantusia henshawi (Granite Night Lizard)

FAMILY: SCINCIDAE

Lygosoma laterale (Ground Skink)
Eumeces fasciatus (Five-lined Skink)
Eumeces inexpectatus (Southeastern Five-lined Skink)
Eumeces laticeps (Broad-headed Skink)
Eumeces obsoletus (Great Plains Skink)
Eumeces multivirgatus (Many-lined Skink)
Eumeces anthracinus (Coal Skink)
Eumeces septentrionalis (Prairie Skink)
Eumeces skiltonianus (Western Skink)

Eumeces gilberti (Greater Brown Skink)
Eumeces gilberti rubricaudatus (Western Red-tailed Skink)
Neoseps reynoldsi (Sand Skink)

FAMILY: TEIIDAE

Cnemidophorus sexlineatus (Six-lined Racerunner)
Cnemidophorus tessellatus (Checkered Whiptail)
Cnemidophorus sacki (Spotted Whiptail)
Cnemidophorus stictogrammus (Arizona Whiptail)
Cnemidophorus tigris (Western Whiptail)

FAMILY: ANGUIDAE

Gerrhonotus coeruleus (California Alligator Lizard)
Gerrhonotus kingi (Arizona Alligator Lizard)
Ophisaurus ventralis (Glass "Snake")

FAMILY: ANNIELLIDAE

Anniella pulchra (Footless Lizard)
Anniella pulchra nigra (Black Footless Lizard)

FAMILY: HELODERMIDAE

Heloderma suspectum (Gila Monster)
Heloderma horridum (Mexican Beaded Lizard)

INDEX